# Covenant Theology and Justification by Faith

# Covenant Theology and Justification by Faith

## The Shepherd Controversy and Its Impacts

Jeong Koo Jeon

Wipf & Stock Publishers
Eugene, Oregon

COVENANT THEOLOGY AND JUSTIFICATION BY FAITH

ISBN: 1-59752-588-X

Manufactured in the U.S.A.

# Table of Contents

# Preface

The book before you provides a comprehensive and critical look at *The Shepherd Controversy* (1975-1982) in respect to covenant, justification by faith, and other related theological issues at Westminster Seminary in Philadelphia and The Philadelphia Presbytery of the Orthodox Presbyterian Church. It also explores contemporary debates on related theological issues. In doing so, I have tried to deal with contemporary discussion on covenant and justification by faith within Reformed and evangelical circles, briefly covering The Auburn Avenue Theology and New Perspective on Paul, especially N.T. Wright.

I received my Ph.D. in Systematic Theology at Westminster Seminary in Philadelphia, and it was during my graduate study (1993-1998), that I was thoroughly aware of *The Shepherd Controversy*, a very heated debate surrounding the teachings of Professor Norman Shepherd. In that regard, my first book *Covenant Theology: John Murray's and Meredith G. Kline's Response to the Historical Development of Federal Theology in Reformed Thought* (1999 & 2004) is a self-consciously anti-Shepherdian or anti-monocovenantal writing, which is a minor revision of my Ph.D. dissertation submitted to the Systematic Theology Department at Westminster Seminary in Philadelphia. I give special thanks to my dissertation advisers, Dr. D. Clair Davis, Dr. Sinclair Ferguson, and Dr. Richard B. Gaffin, Jr., who was the chair of the Systematic Theology Department. Their patient advice and guidance immensely helped me in better forming my thinking and the direction of my thesis. It is worth mentioning, however, that Dr. Ferguson, as my second adviser, and I disagreed on the distinction between Law and Gospel in relation to justification 'by faith alone' (*sola fide*). I am also very thankful to Dr. W. Robert Godfrey, a leading Protestant Reformation scholar who taught me the importance of the Protestant evangelical distinction between Law and Gospel in the 16th century Reformation, and who wrote a wonderful Forward for my first book.

In the midst of my graduate research and writing, I discovered that the Shepherd Controversy arose as Professor Shepherd and others in Westminster Theological Seminary in Philadelphia rejected the Protestant evangelical distinction between Law and Gospel in relation to covenant, justification by faith, election and other related theological issues. In the milieu of the theological controversy, I received my degree in defending the evangelical distinction between Law and Gospel in relation to justification 'by faith alone' (*sola fide*) from the theologies of John Calvin to John Murray and Meredith G. Kline in the Reformed tradition, including the Westminster Standards (1643-1648), although it was not an easy contour to do so.

This current book directly deals and encounters with The Shepherd Controversy and contemporary debate on covenant and justification and other related theological issues. I classify Professor Shepherd and other theologians, who have supported Professor Shepherd's theology directly or indirectly, as Reformed monocovenantalists because they unanimously reject the Protestant evangelical distinction between Law and Gospel in their analysis of covenant and justification by faith, as well as the Pauline soteriology. Furthermore, I classify their theology as the Union with Christ School because they apply exclusively the concept of 'the union with Christ' (*unio cum Christo*) without referring to or by rejecting the distinction between Law and Gospel in their analysis of Calvin's and the Pauline soteriology.

It is my belief that many scholars, pastors, seminarians, and lay people have unknowingly fallen into Reformed monocovenantalism due to the heavy influence of the Union with Christ School scholars, who have been at the forefront of the Reformed theology and scholarship for several decades on a global scale. It is my historical theological conviction that no one can interpret the Protestant Reformation consensus on justification 'by faith alone' (*sola fide*) and salvation 'by grace alone' (*sola gratia*) between Luther and Calvin without reckoning the distinction between Law and Gospel, which was the vital underlying hermeneutical and theological principle of the Reformation. I argue that Calvin as a covenant theologian faithfully apply the Pauline distinction between Law and Gospel in his depiction of justification by faith alone while he embraces all the soteriological blessings, including divine election under the rubric of union with Christ.

I never studied theology under Professor Shepherd. In the process of writing the current book, I tried to reach Professor Shepherd to gain a more comprehensive knowledge of his theology through direct personal discussion. Unfortunately, this did not happen. In the present book, I provide a comprehensive critique not only of Professor Shepherd's theology, but also to that of some of my former revered professors. They are globally well-known and respected scholars, theologians, preachers, and writers in conservative Reformed and evangelical circles. I still revere them as my former professors. In that sense, I hope that my readers may read my critique not as a personal one but a theological one. It is my hope that this book may, in some way, serve as yet another catalyst for rethinking the vital importance of the distinction between Law and Gospel in understanding the Protestant Reformation and the Pauline soteriology, and most importantly the Gospel itself.

Until the last moment of preparing present book, I was very hesitant whether to publish it or not because of the nature of this theological controversy and since the discussion compelled me to provide a comprehensive critique of my former revered professors. Ultimately, however, I decided to publish it. My goal in publishing the present book is to clarify the massive confusion surrounding this contemporary debate on covenant and justification by faith, and to provide a comprehensive picture for future generations of Reformed and evangelical scholars, pastors, and laity. I hope to further develop these ideas in my next book *Covenant Theology vs. The New Perspectives on Paul* if somehow I have made any errors or misinterpretations in my critical analysis presented in this book. It is my sincere hope that my readers may read this book with sincere heart and care, thinking about the glory of God and the glory of the Kingdom of God. May the Lord richly bless my readers! *Soli Deo gloria!!!*

# Introduction

Norman Shepherd's publication of *The Call of Grace* in 2000[1] fueled and revived a theological controversy in Reformed and evangelical communities. He was a systematic theology professor at Westminster Theological Seminary in Philadelphia (1963-1982). The Shepherd Controversy over his views of covenant and justification by faith lasted for seven years at the seminary and the Philadelphia Presbytery of the Orthodox Presbyterian Church (1975-1982).[2] Ultimately, he was removed from his teaching position by the recommendation of the board of the seminary against his own will and that of his supporters. However, scholars and others who were involved in this controversy were evenly divided with respect to Shepherd's views. Shepherd and his supporters have consistently

---

[1] Norman Shepherd, *The Call of Grace: How the Covenant Illuminates Salvation and Evangelism* (Phillipsburg, NJ: P&R Publishing, 2000).

[2] For a comprehensive and critical analysis of the Shepherd Controversy (1975-82) on covenant and justification by faith and other related issues, see A. Donald MacLeod, *W. Stanford Reid: An Evangelical Calvinist in the Academy* (Montreal & Kingston / London / Ithaca: McGill-Queen's University Press, 2004), 257-79; RCUS, "Report of the Special Committee to Study Justification in Light of the Current Justification Controversy: Presented to the 258th Synod of the Reformed Church of the United States," May 10-13, 2004 (http://www.trinityrcus.com/Articles/reportshepherdl.htm); O. Palmer Robertson, *The Current Justification Controversy* (Unicoi, Tennessee: The Trinity Foundation), 5-107; Robert M. Zens, "Professor Norman Shepherd on Justification: A Critique" (Th.M. thesis, Dallas Theological Seminary, 1981).

argued that his views of the covenant and the doctrine of justification by faith are perfectly harmonious with the Protestant Reformation view of the doctrine of justification by faith and the Reformed understanding of the covenant. They have consistently insisted that Shepherd's theology is compatible with the Westminster Standards and the Pauline soteriology. In that sense, I think that it is unfair to point to Shepherd alone when providing a theological critique of the views associated with the Shepherd Controversy. Recently, many scholars and pastors have written critical pieces opposing Shepherd's theology, and the majority of these critiques focus solely on Shepherd. I suggest that the Shepherd Controversy on covenant and justification by faith must be *collectively* evaluated because prominent scholars at Westminster Seminary in Philadelphia have supported Shepherd's theology even to the present time. In these pages, I will argue that the Shepherd Controversy (1975-1982) at Westminster Seminary in Philadelphia was inevitable because of the growing consensus of monocovenantalism among the followers of John Murray after his retirement in 1966. Reformed monocovenantalism is a distinctive theological movement, exclusively emphasizing union with Christ in its soteriology and rejecting the antithesis between Law and Gospel. In doing so, they applied a 'sympathetic theological method,' arguing that their theology is well harmonized with Calvin's theology, the Westminster Standards, and Reformed theology.[3]

---

[3] Several scholars, pastors and others have responded critically to Shepherd's new theology. By and large, however, their criticism is limited to Shepherd's theology alone, although some scholars evaluate it from a collective perspective. For critical evaluation on Shepherd's new theology, see E. Calvin Beisner, "The Current Challenge," *Modern Reformation* 13/4 (July/August, 2004), 17-22; Michael Horton, "Déjà Vu All Over Again," *Modern Reformation* 13/4 (July/August, 2004), 23-30; The Faculty of Westminster Seminary California, "Our Testimony on Justification: A Summary of the Statement from the Faculty of Westminster Seminary California," *Modern Reformation* 13/4 (July/August, 2004), 37; W. Robert Godfrey, "Westminster Seminary, the Doctrine of Justification, and the Reformed Confessions," in *The Pattern of Sound Doctrine: Systematic Theology at the Westminster Seminaries: Essays in Honor of Robert B. Strimple*, ed. David VanDrunen (Phillipsburg, NJ: P & R Publishing, 2004), 127-48; Mark W. Karlberg, *The Changing of the Guard: Westminster Theological Seminary* (Unicoi, TN: The Trinity Foundation, 2001); idem, *Gospel Grace: The Modern-day Controversy* (Eugene, OR: Wipf and Stock Publishers, 2003); David Linden, Review of "Justification by Faith Alone," by Norman Shepherd (www.grebeweb.com/linden/shepherd_review.htm); Cornelis P. Venema,

It is my thesis that Shepherd's and his supporters' theology of covenant and justification by faith not only opposes the Protestant Reformation principle of justification by faith alone, but also is inharmonious with the Westminster Standards and Pauline soteriology. The most fundamental problem of his new theology lies in his rejection of the distinction between Law and Gospel as a hermeneutical tool for interpreting the doctrine of justification 'by faith alone' (*sola fide*), which was the Protestant Reformation consensus between Martin Luther and John Calvin. Moreover, his rejection of the Law and Gospel distinction led him to deny the distinction between the covenant of works and the covenant of grace, which has been a key hermeneutical principle for Reformed orthodox theology in interpreting the *historia salutis* (redemptive history) and the *ordo salutis* (order of salvation) covenantally and eschatologically. As a result, his new theology inevitably falls into covenant-legalism, which inevitably implies a denial of the doctrines of God's sovereign grace, double predestination, and the substitutionary view of atonement.

It is my contention that Shepherd and his supporters misread historical theology by insisting that the antithesis between Law and Gospel in relation to the doctrine of justification by faith alone was distinctively and solely a Lutheran idea during the sixteenth century Protestant Reformation. Their misreading of historical theology has had a devastating theological impact upon Shepherd, his supporters, and his followers. In this important matter, I will demonstrate that the antithesis between Law and Gospel in relation to the doctrine of justification by faith alone has always been a vital hermeneutical reference point in all Reformed orthodox theology since the Protestant Reformation, including *The Westminster Standards (1643-1648)*. In this respect, I will argue that justification by faith alone must stand and fall together with the antithesis between Law and Gospel as an important hermeneutical tool.

Moreover, I will suggest that Shepherd's and his supporters' monocovenantalism, in rejecting this antithesis between Law and Gospel

---

Review of *The Call of Grace: How the Covenant Illuminates Salvation and Evangelism*, by Norman Shepherd *Mid-America Journal of Theology* 13 (2002): 232-48; Rowland S. Ward, *God & Adam: Reformed Theology and the Creation Covenant* (Wantrina, Australia: New Melbourne Press, 2003), 187-92; Guy Prentiss Waters, *Justification and the New Perspectives on Paul* (Phillipsburg, NJ: P & R Publishing, 2004), 204-12.

along with the antithesis between the covenant of works and the covenant of grace, led to the opening of the floodgate to ecumenical theology, including Roman Catholicism, neo-orthodox theology, the Auburn Avenue Theology, and the New Perspective on Paul movement represented by E.P. Sanders and his followers, in which the antithesis between Law and Gospel is denied in their understanding of the Gospel and theological system.

# I.
## The Rise of Monocovenantalism

### A. Karl Barth's Existential Monocovenantalism

The 20th century was the century of the rise of monocovenantalism. Its chief spokesman was the great architect of neo-orthodox theology, Karl Barth. He thought that the greatest barrier in the road to ecumenical theology, embracing Roman Catholic theology and others, is the distinction between Law and Gospel. During the Protestant Reformation this dichotomy was a common denominator between Luther and Calvin in their depiction of the doctrine of justification by faith alone. Calvinists after Calvin's theological pattern developed the distinction between the covenant of works and the covenant of grace, which ever since has been a vital hermeneutical principle of Reformed hermeneutics and theology. But through the perspective of Barth's existential neo-orthodox theological program, the distinction between Law and Gospel along with the antithesis between the covenant of works and the covenant of grace falls into the category of dualism and is viewed as directly contradictory to his idea of Christomonistic grace. This is the reason for his harsh criticism of this perceived dualism. Certainly, there is no place for the antithesis between Law and Gospel in Barth's Christomonistic existential theology. Therefore, he radically alters the theological program, proposing *law in the gospel or gospel in the law* as a substitute for the Protestant Reformation hermeneutical principle of the antithesis between Law and Gospel: "In Scripture we do not find the Law alongside the Gospel but in the Gospel, and therefore the holiness of God is not side by side with but in His grace, and His wrath is not separate from but in His love."[1]

No doubt, Barth was in a sense correct: we can certainly embrace ecumenical theology if we are willing to reject the distinction between Law and Gospel in the Barthian fashion. But consequently Reformed theology itself is shattered if we reject the distinction between Law and Gospel along with the distinction between the covenant of works and the covenant of grace. For Barth, the covenant of works in the prelapsarian Adamic condition is an original universalism:

> Their doctrine of a purely intertrinitarian pact did not enable them to give an unequivocal or binding answer to the question of the form of the eternal divine decree as the beginning of all things. The result was that for all their loyalty to Scripture they inherited the notion that the covenant of grace fulfilled and revealed in history in Jesus Christ was perhaps only a secondary and subsequent divine arrangement (the foundation and history of a religion?) and not the beginning of all the ways of God. Their view of the covenant became dualistic. The idea of a basic and always determinative and concurrent covenant of nature or works was superimposed on their conception of the covenant of grace. Yet this could have been avoided–even though as children of their time they were exposed to the temptation of humanism–if they could have determined to know the eternal and therefore the only basis of the divine work in the work itself, in its temporal occurrence, to know the eternal divine Logos in His incarnation. And on this basis they might well have overcome the other weaknesses in their doctrine: the abandonment of an original universalism in the conception of the covenant; and finally the radical historicism of their understanding of Scripture.[2]

---

[1] Karl Barth, *Church Dogmatics*, trans. G. W. Bromiley, vol. 2/1 (Edinburgh: T. & T. Clark, 1974), 362-63.

[2] Barth, *Church Dogmatics*, vol. 4/1, 66.

Unfortunately, the Barthian *law in grace or gospel in law* idea merged into the twentieth century evangelical and Reformed theological worlds, directly and indirectly, and still influences them in a powerful manner.

Shepherd and his supporters in the Westminster School are not Barthians. In many ways, they are conservative Reformed theologians. However, they share a similar idea in their rejection of the antithesis between Law and Gospel in their reformulation and reinterpretation of covenant and justification by faith alone. In this regard, they have no final rejoinder to the Barthian *law in grace* existential theological program, because they reject the antithesis between Law and Gospel both directly and indirectly. In this unfortunate theological construction, there is no room for the doctrines of double predestination, a substitutionary view of atonement, sovereign grace in salvation, and justification by faith alone. In a word, all theological backbones of the Protestant Reformation and Reformed theology collapse.

## B. Reformed Rejection of the Antithesis between Law and Gospel

### 1. Calvin, the Westminster Standards, and Murray against the Union with Christ School

In many ways, Shepherd and his supporters in the Westminster School are Murrayans. Shepherd began to teach systematic theology in 1963 at his *alma mater*, Westminster Seminary in Philadelphia, under the blessing and guidance of his well-respected predecessor, John Murray. Murray was a Reformed biblico-systematic theologian, whose contribution to biblico-systematic theology is immense. He was heavily influenced by his Old Princeton professor, Geerhardus Vos, who self-consciously developed biblico-systematic theology under the rubrics of the distinction between the covenant of works and the covenant of grace, applying it covenantally, redemptive-historically, and eschatologically. Murray rejected the terminology of the covenant of works in his biblico-systematic theology. However, his theology is still compatible with the distinction between the covenant of works and covenant of grace, because his rejection of the covenant of works is not substantial. Most importantly, Murray maintained the distinction between Law and Gospel in his exposition of justification by faith alone. It is the most important reason why he does not fall into monocovenantalism, whereas his immediate successor Shepherd and his supporters do. Moreover, he did not artificially separate Luther and Calvin in their expositions of doctrine of justification by faith alone, because he correctly perceived that it was the Protestant Reformation consensus.

After Murray's retirement in 1966, a questionable hypothesis was growing and forming among some Murrayans–a hypothesis that the distinction between Law and Gospel was distinctively a Lutheran idea during the Protestant Reformation not shared by Calvin. Thus, consciously and unconsciously, they began to reject the adoption of the distinction between Law and Gospel in their theological system, and they began to justify their novel analysis by saying that Calvin did not maintain the distinction between Law and Gospel in his exposition of justification by faith because he was a covenant theologian who emphasized the covenant conditionality against Luther. Therefore, I maintain that Shepherd and his supporters within the Westminster Seminary should be considered as a *New Westminster School*, because there was no one among the Old Princeton and Old Westminster theologians who would reject the distinction between Law and Gospel, especially in the exposition of justification by faith alone. Unanimously, they conceived that it was the Protestant Reformation consensus. No one questioned it until Shepherd and his supporters began to attack the distinction between Law and Gospel, arguing it as an antinomian hermeneutical principle.[3]

In studying Protestant Reformation theology in the sixteenth century, it is very important to notice that Calvin did not reject Luther's distinction between Law and Gospel in his exposition of justification by faith alone. In fact, the genius of Calvin's theology lies precisely in his adaptation of the antithesis between Law and Gospel, while he also applies union with Christ as another concrete hermeneutical tool to interpret Pauline

---

[3] In the Reformed tradition, historical theologians and systematic theologians unanimously have recognized that justification 'by faith alone' (*sola fide*) in light of the antithesis between Law and Gospel was the Protestant Reformation consensus between Luther and Calvin. I am greatly indebted to them in that regard. And I think that it is a correct historical theological assessment. I have documented it in Jeong Koo Jeon, *Covenant Theology: John Murray's and Meredith G. Kline's Response to the Historical Development of Federal Theology in Reformed Thought* (Lanham, MD: University Press of America, 2004), 15-16.

soteriology. Calvin applied two hermeneutical tools in his depiction of justification by faith alone: they are the antithesis between Law and Gospel, and 'union with Christ' (*unio cum Christo*). I argue that no one can understand Calvin's analysis of Pauline soteriology and justification by faith alone without referring to these two hermeneutical tools. In fact, it is clear that Calvin was not able to discuss the doctrine of justification by faith alone without referring to these two principles:

> Still they do not observe that in the contrast between the righteousness of the law and of the gospel, which Paul elsewhere introduces, all works are excluded, whatever title may grace them [Gal. 3:11-12]. For he teaches that this is the righteousness of the law, that he who has fulfilled what the law commands should obtain salvation; but this is the righteousness of faith, to believe that Christ died and rose again [Rom. 10:5,9].[4]

Likewise, to say that Calvin rejected the distinction between Law and Gospel in his depiction of justification by faith is a drastic misreading of Calvin's theology as a whole. Once again, Calvin unmistakably and irrefutably affirmed the Pauline hermeneutical tools, namely the distinction between Law and Gospel, and 'union with Christ' (*unio cum Christo*):

> For in comparing the law and the gospel in the letter to the Romans he says: "the righteousness that is of the law" is such that "the man who practices these things will live by them" [Rom. 10:5]. But the "righteousness that is of faith" [Rom. 10:6] announces salvation "if you believe in your heart and confess with your mouth that Jesus is Lord and that the Father raised him from the dead" [Rom. 10:9 p.]. Do you see how he makes this the distinction between law and gospel: that the former attributes righteousness to works, the latter bestows free righteousness apart from the help of works? This is an important passage, and one that can extricate us from many difficulties if we understand that that righteousness which is given us through the gospel has been freed of all conditions of the law. Here is the reason why he so often

---

[4] John Calvin, *Institutes of the Christian Religion*, ed. John T. McNeil, trans. Ford Lewis Battles, *Library of Christian Classics*, vols. 20-21 (Philadelphia, PA: The Westminster Press, 1975), 3.11.14

opposes the promise to the law, as things mutually contradictory: "If the inheritance is by the law, it is no longer by promise" [Gal. 3:18]; and passages in the same chapter that express this idea. Now, to be sure, the law itself has its own promises. Therefore, in the promises of the gospel there must be something distinct and different unless we would admit that the comparison is inept. But what sort of difference will this be, other than that the gospel promises are free and dependent solely upon God's mercy, while the promises of the law depend upon the condition of works?[5]

As we examine Shepherd's and his supporters' rejection of the antithesis between Law and Gospel, we need to be reminded constantly that Calvin affirmed it along with union with Christ as two hermeneutical principles in the analysis of the Pauline concepts of justification by faith alone and salvation.

Tracing the exact origins of monocovenantalism in the Westminster School poses a formidable challenge. I personally think that Shepherd and several of his supporters adopted monocovenantalism from a famous Dutch Reformed theologian, G. C. Berkouwer. Shepherd studied theology under the supervision of Berkouwer while he taught at the Westminster Seminary in Philadelphia. Berkouwer rejected the antithesis between Law and Gospel in the depiction of justification by faith, and adopted the Barthian *law in grace* idea uncritically in his own theological system. For example, Berkouwer writes:

> Barth contends that 'in Scripture we do not find the Law alongside the Gospel but *in* the Gospel.' Therefore he reverses the usual order of 'law and Gospel' and speaks of 'the Gospel and the law.' He recognizes that *within* this sequence there is room for reflecting on 'the law and the Gospel.' Nevertheless, the right accent is preserved only when we speak of the *Gospel first*.
>
> This reversal of the sequence has everything to do with the inner structure of Barth's theology. Negatively, we find a radical antilegalism in Barth - for Barth is against the law as a means of salvation. Positively, we find the triumph and priority of grace.[6]

---

[5] Ibid., 3.11.17.

[6] G. C. Berkouwer, *Studies in Dogmatics: Sin*, trans. Philip C. Holtrop (Grand Rapids, MI: Eerdmans Publishing Company, 1971), 204.

Adopting Berkouwer's rejection of the distinction between Law and Gospel, Shepherd began to reinterpret Protestant Reformation theology. In particular, Shepherd argues that Luther's distinction between Law and Gospel is an antinomian concept. It is very important here to note Shepherd's separation of Luther and Calvin in the doctrine of justification. The primary theological reason to separate them is the issue of the distinction between Law and Gospel. Following Berkouwer, Shepherd rejects the distinction between Law and Gospel in the doctrine of justification. However, the distinctive nature of Shepherd's rejection lies in separating Luther and Calvin:

> We are profoundly grateful for the progress that was made by the Reformation. We were led into a more biblical understanding of the way of salvation. Nonetheless, unresolved issues remain. There have been long-standing differences between adherents of the historic Lutheran and Reformed confessions. That is evident especially in their different attitudes toward the law. The law can serve to reveal and convince us of our own sin, but Lutherans fear that making the commandments a rule for Christian living will confuse law and gospel. They fear that it will confuse salvation by grace with salvation by works.[7]

Shepherd's historical theological reading, especially on Calvin, decisively separates his new theology, and that of his supporters and followers, from the Reformed tradition. Shepherd's and his supporters' thesis is important because they use it as their main theological reason for denying the distinction between Law and Gospel in their radical reinterpretation of covenant, justification, predestination, and other theological issues. In his recent writing, he clearly rejects the distinction between Law and Gospel. His monocovenantalism clearly denies it: "To summarize, we can look at law and gospel from a covenantal perspective in two ways, namely, in terms of the history of redemption (*historia salutis*) and in terms of the application of redemption (*ordo salutis*). In neither of these ways are law and gospel antithetically opposed."[8]

---

[7] Shepherd, *The Call of Grace*, 5.

[8] Norman Shepherd, "Law and Gospel in Covenantal Perspective: The Unity of God's Salvific Plan" (http://www.christianculture.com/cgilocal/npublisher/viewnews.cgi?category=3&id=1100539305).

On the other hand, Shepherd constructs a great chasm between Luther and Calvin on the doctrine of justification because he fails to see the distinction between Law and Gospel clearly expressed in Calvin's depiction of justification by faith. In this sense, Shepherd's new theology is fundamentally different from the theology of Calvin, the Westminster Standards, Murray, and other orthodox Reformed theologians:

> There were significant differences between Luther and Calvin when it came to the nature of justifying faith, differences that still play a role in the discussion today. The Lutheran doctrine of justification by faith alone excludes the Reformed doctrine of justification by a penitent and obedient faith. But Luther and Calvin were agreed that justification was not an infusion of righteousness as Rome taught. Justification is the remission of sin on the ground of the righteousness of Christ imputed to the believer. This righteousness was his suffering and death for us, what later theologians called his passive obedience. The righteousness of Christ secures the remission of sin.[9]

By contrast John Murray, Shepherd's predecessor at the Westminster School, did not separate Luther and Calvin on the doctrine of justification. This is consistent with the classical interpretation of historical theology inasmuch as Murray correctly conceived that Luther and Calvin maintained the distinction between Law and Gospel in their depiction of justification by faith alone, no matter how different their theology:

> It may be safe to say that the greatest event for Christendom in the last 1500 years was the Protestant Reformation. What was the spark that lit the flame of evangelical passion? It was, by the grace of God, the discovery on the part of Luther, stricken with a sense of his estrangement from God and feeling in his inmost soul the stings of his wrath and the remorse of a terrified conscience, of the true and only way whereby a man can be just with God. To him the truth of justification by free grace through faith lifted him from the depths of the forebodings of

---

[9] Norman Shepherd, "Justification by Works in Reformed Theology," in *Backbone of the Bible: Covenant in Contemporary Perspective*, ed. P. Andrew Sandlin (Nacogdoches, TX: Covenant Media Press, 2004), 111.

hell to the ecstasy of peace with God and the hope of glory. If there is one thing the Church needs today it is the republication with faith and passion of the presuppositions of the doctrine of justification and the reapplication of this, the article of a standing or falling Church. 'Being justified freely by his grace through the redemption that is in Christ Jesus: Whom God hath set forth to be a propitiation through faith in his blood, to declare his righteousness for the remission of sins that are past, through the forbearance of God; To declare, I say, at this time his righteousness: that he might be just, and the justifier of him which believeth in Jesus' (Romans 3:24-26).[10]

One of the most important supporters of Shepherd's new theology during the seven years controversy and until the present day is Richard B. Gaffin, Jr. Those who have revered and respected Gaffin's Reformed orthodoxy and profound scholarship may wonder why he has consistently supported Shepherd's new theology on covenant and justification by faith. Gaffin endorsed Shepherd's controversial book *The Call of Grace* on the back cover: "This lucid and highly readable study provides valuable instruction on what it means to live in covenant with God. God's covenant is the only way of life that fully honors both the absolute, all-embracing sovereignty of his saving grace and the full, uninhibited activity of his people. *The Call of Grace* should benefit anyone concerned about biblical growth in Christian life and witness."[11] Gaffin's endorsement on the back cover alone, however, is not decisive theological evidence that he shares monocovenantalism with Shepherd. Rather, I argue that he has consistently supported Shepherd's new theology as compatible with Calvin, the Westminster Standards, Reformed theology, and Pauline soteriology.

In fact, I would like to carefully suggest here that Gaffin may actually be the primary author of monocovenantalism rejecting the distinction between Law and Gospel at the New Westminster School. The monocovenantal argument first appeared not in Shepherd's writing, but in Gaffin's dissertation, completed in 1969 at the Westminster Seminary. It is important to note that his dissertation was not written under the supervision

---

[10] John Murray, *Collected Writings of John Murray: Selected Lectures in Systematic Theology* (The Banner of Truth, 1977), 2:203.

[11] Shepherd, *The Call of Grace*, written in the back cover.

of Murray but of Shepherd and others.[12] In 1966, Murray retired from the seminary, and returned to his home country Scotland. Gaffin's dissertation was an excellent piece of writing about Pauline soteriology, reflecting that he was heavily influenced by his revered predecessor Murray and the Old Princeton biblical theologian Vos, to whom he dedicated his dissertation. He argues that 'union with Christ' (*unio cum Christo*) must be a single hermeneutical tool applied to interpret Pauline soteriology and eschatology. He brilliantly shows that the Pauline eschatological tension between *already but not yet* is an important component that traditional Reformed theologians by and large have ignored or bypassed. Union with Christ in his life, death, and resurrection through faith, he argues, is the central motif in Pauline soteriology. In his discussion of the Pauline 'order of salvation' (*ordo salutis*) and redemptive history (*historia salutis*), he suggests that the traditional Reformed concept of the order of salvation (the *ordo salutis*) is significantly flawed. Here, we need to be reminded that Calvin and other Reformed theologians, including Murray, used two hermeneutical tools to interpret the Pauline soteiology and the doctrine of justification by faith alone. These two tools are union with Christ and the antithesis between Law and Gospel. However, Gaffin viewed the antithesis between Law and Gospel, traditionally applied by the Reformed theologians in their

---

[12] Cf. Richard B. Gaffin, Jr., "Resurrection and Redemption: A Study in Pauline Soteriology" (Th.D. diss., Westminster Theological Seminary, 1969). Surprisingly, David VanDrunen, who replaced Robert Strimple at Westminster Seminary in California as a systematic theology professor does not notice Gaffin's theological struggle, manifested in his *magnum opus, Resurrection and Redemption.* VanDrunen, as Strimple's replacement, is very critical of Shepherd's new theology. However, he mistakenly places Murray and Gaffin in the same tradition, and he mistakenly writes that Gaffin wrote his dissertation under Murray: "Perhaps more illuminating than what these men [Murray, Gaffin, and Strimple] did not write is what they did write, which as much as anything else was biblical exegesis. Murray's *opus magnum* was almost certainly his two-volume commentary on Romans. Even his (arguably) best systematics work, *The Imputation of Adam's Sin*, is to a great extent a rigorous exegetical study of one passage, Romans 5:12-19. Gaffin's first, and probably best-known, monograph, *Resurrection and Redemption*, originally written as a systematic dissertation under Murray at Westminster, is essentially a study in Pauline soteriology. Its application to the systematics themes of union with Christ and the *ordo salutis* are brief and rather tentative." David VanDrunen, "A System of Theology?: The Centrality of Covenant for Westminster Systematics," in *The Pattern of Sound Doctrine: Systematic Theology at the Westminster Seminaries (Essays in Honor of Robert B. Strimple)*, ed. David VanDrunen (Phillipsburg, NJ: P & R Publishing, 2004), 201.

understanding of Pauline soteriology and justification by faith alone, to be problematic. Thus, applying his own 'sympathetic critical method,' he self-consciously began to reject or ignore adopting the antithesis between Law and Gospel in his understanding of the Pauline theology.[13] I argue that this is a decisive departing point of Gaffin's biblico-systematic theology from the Protestant Reformation and Reformed theology as a whole. In Gaffin's "sympathetic critical method," there is no place for the antithesis

---

[13] In fact, Gaffin borrowed the word, 'sympathetic critical' method from the Dutch Reformed theologian, Klass Schilder, and began to use the expression from 1994. See Richard B. Gaffin Jr., "The Vitality of Reformed Dogmatics," in *The Vitality of Reformed Theology: Proceedings of the International Theological Congress June 20-24th 1994, Noordwijkerhout, The Netherlands*. eds. J.M. Batteau, J.W. Maris, and K. Veling (Kampen: Uitgeverij Kok, 1994), 21. Tim Trumper as a replacement of Ferguson in systematic theology department at Westminster Seminary in Philadelphia wrote a long review article on my book *Covenant Theology* although he does not teach there any more. Overall, it is a favorable review article on my book. Interestingly, he defines the hermeneutics and theology of Westminster Seminary in Philadelphia as 'constructive Calvinism,' adopting the thought pattern of Gaffin. I think that he wrote his review article to counter the critics who are against the Union with Christ School scholars, led by Gaffin. However, it is evident that Trumper fundamentally misread the theology of the Union with Christ School, identifying it as constructive Calvinism with a positive note. The most crucial point is whether the constructive Calvinists accept and apply the antithesis between Law and Gospel in their depiction of covenant and justification by faith. In a word, they do not do it. However, Trumper ambiguously states as if they accept and apply the antithesis between Law and Gospel with some improvements. In that sense, his review article is not helpful to clarify theological issues in contemporary debate on covenant and justification by faith. In concluding remarks, he mistakenly argues giving a false impression to his readers as if the constructive Calvinists adopt the distinction between Law and Gospel: "All in all, then, Jeon's work is useful. It gives a through overview of an important debate within our tradition. As his sympathies evidently lie with Kline, speaking methodologically mine lie with Murray, although I remain open to benefit from Kline. What criticisms I have made of Kline have been intended to reduce the level of acrimony among Westminster Calvinists and not to aggravate it. But there can only be genuine unity in the defense of federal theology if it is made to rest on the Law-Gospel antithesis itself and not on a covenant of works (p. 329). Therein lies the issue. Our response will be determined by whether we consider a covenant of works to be the regulating principle of federal theology. But this is an investigation for another day." Tim J.R. Trumper, "Covenant Theology and Constructive Calvinism," in Review of *Covenant Theology: John Murray's and Meredith G. Kline's Response to the Historical Development of Federal Theology in Reformed Thought*, by Jeong Koo Jeon *Westminster Theological Journal* (Fall, 2002): 404.

between Law and Gospel in his exposition of the Pauline theology. As a result, he departs from Calvin, Bavinck, Vos, and Murray, the very same people with whom he wanted to identify. In his indirect rejection of the antithesis between Law and Gospel in his interpretation of Pauline soteriology, it is evident that Gaffin was heavily influenced by the two most important contemporary Dutch Reformed theologians, Berkouwer and Riddervos:

> The traditional *ordo salutis* lacks the exclusively eschatological air which pervades the entire Pauline soteriology. Or, to put it the other way around, the former point of view amounts to a definite de-eschatologization of Paul's outlook. For him soteriology *is* eschatology. All soteric experience derives from solidarity in Christ's resurrection and involves existence in the new creation age, inaugurated by his resurrection. As Romans 8:30 reflects, the present as well as the future of the believer is conceived of eschatologically. This understanding of present Christian existence as an (eschatological) tension between resurrection realized and yet to be realized is totally foreign to the traditional *ordo salutis*. In the latter, justification, adoption, sanctification (and regeneration) are deprived of any eschatological significance and any really integral connection with the future. Eschatology enters the *ordo salutis* only as glorification, standing at a more or less isolated distance in the future, is discussed within the locus on 'last things.'[14]

Certainly, Gaffin's emphasis on the importance of eschatological tension between *already but not yet* in light of the Pauline eschatology and soteriology is an important Pauline concept. Yet, his critical posture against the traditional understanding of the *ordo salutis* reflects his posture against the antithesis between Law and Gospel as a hermentuical tool in the exposition of the Pauline doctrine of justification by faith alone (*sola fide*) and salvation by grace alone (*sola gratia*). Thus, according to his sympathetic critical method, Reformed theologians such as Bavinck, Berkhof, Hodge, Kuyper, and Murray come under serious scrutiny because they unanimously applied an important hermeneutical tool, the antithesis

---

[14] Richard B. Gaffin Jr., *Resurrection and Redemption: A Study in Paul's Soteriology* (Phillipsburg, NJ: P&R Publishing, 1987), 137-38.

between Law and Gospel in their exposition of Pauline soteriology and the doctrine of justification by faith alone:

> Nothing distinguishes the traditional *ordo salutis* more than its insistence that the justification, adoption, and sanctification which occur at the inception of the application of redemption are separate acts. If our interpretation is correct, Paul views them not as distinct acts but as distinct aspects of a single act. The significant difference here is not simply that Paul does not have the problem that faces the traditional *ordo salutis* in having, by its very structure, to establish the pattern of priorities (temporal? logical? causal?) which obtains among these acts.[15]

Gaffin's critical position against the traditional *ordo salutis* implicitly reflects his fundamental opposition to the distinction between Law and Gospel without explicitly mentioning it, as his exclusive emphasis on union with Christ in the Pauline eschatology and soteriology strongly suggests:

> The structure and problematics of the traditional *ordo salutis* prohibits making an unequivocal statement concerning that on which Paul stakes everything in the application of redemption, namely union with the resurrected Christ. The first and, in the final analysis, the only question for the Pauline *ordo* concerns the point at which and the conditions under which incorporation with the life-giving Spirit takes place. And the pointedness of this question is not blunted nor is its centrality obscured by introducing considerations deriving from solidarity with Christ in the design and accomplishment of redemption.[16]

Certainly, Gaffin's exclusive emphasis on the union with Christ in his analysis of the Pauline soteriology and eschatology is the most important theological departure that ever happened at Westminster Seminary in Philadelphia. For this reason, I suggest that his dissertation in 1969 must be considered as the inauguration of the *Union with Christ School* at Westminster Seminary in Philadelphia. Gaffin is a much more concrete

---

[15] Ibid., 138.
[16] Ibid., 139.

theologian than Shepherd. Gaffin does not agree with Shepherd at each and every point of his depiction of covenant, justification by faith, and other closely related theological issues. However, Gaffin does agree with Shepherd in the rejection of the Pauline antithesis between Law and Gospel. This, I suggest, is the most important reason he has consistently supported and defended Shepherd's new theology on covenant and justification since the outbreak of theological controversy in 1975.[17]

---

[17] Cf. Richard B. Gaffin Jr., "Resurrection and Redemption: A Study in Pauline Soteriology" (Th.D. diss., Westminster Theological Seminary, 1969). Nowadays, growing numbers of scholars, pastors, and seminarians fall into monocovenantalism, promoted and expounded by Union with Christ School scholars, represented by Gaffin. The most confusing element of Union with Christ School movement is that they appeal to Calvin's soteriology, injecting a radically reinterpreted concept of 'union with Christ' (*unio cum Christo*) to Calvin's soteriology. The common historical theological error for them is that they ignore or reject Calvin's concrete hermeneutical tool, namely the distinction between Law and Gospel. One of the representative examples is Craig Carpenter. Relying heavily on Gaffin's monocovenantalism where he exclusively emphasizes the concept of union with Christ, without referring to the distinction between Law and Gospel in Pauline soteriology, Carpenter also exclusively emphasizes the concept of union with Christ in the exposition of Calvin's doctrine of justification by faith. In doing so, he also denies justification by faith alone as a common consensus between Luther and Calvin: "Just as his teaching on the real presence in the Lord's Supper is not a mere *via media* between Luther and Zwingli but possesses a scripturally faithful uniqueness, Calvin's doctrine of justification reveals his distinctive–perhaps even incisive–scriptural insight into this important issue of soteriology. Put differently, Calvin does not develop his view of justification simply over against the errors of others; rather, when he combats the errors of others he does so based on his definite view of justification. And his positive view sees justification as a key element or benefits in the soteric complex that brings a believer into an indissoluble union and communion with Christ." Craig B. Carpenter, "A Question of Union with Christ? Calvin and Trent on Justification," *Westminster Theological Journal* 64 (Fall, 2002): 371. Carpenter completely ignores or bypasses the concept of the distinction between Law and Gospel, which is a vital hermeneutical tool along with the concept of union with Christ in Calvin's soteriology. In doing so, he makes Calvin a monocovenantalist, perhaps without knowing it. Again, Carpenter echoes Gaffin's exclusive emphasis on union with Christ in his exposition of Calvin's soteriology: "Justification and sanctification, imputation and infusion, Christ and the Holy Spirit – these are as inseparable in salvation as the sun's light is from its heat. God's monergistic formation of faith in the Christian unites him irrefragably to Christ, who is his righteousness, sanctification, and redemption. To embrace Christ in the Gospel is to embrace every redemptive blessing purchased by him as well. Justification and sanctification are distinct soteric aspects, or benefits, of one's union with Christ.... Calvin's

Here, we need to reflect Sinclair B. Ferguson's thought and his role in the Shepherd Controversy. He has been a well-respected Reformed theologian, a prolific writer, and a great preacher. I consider preaching as the most gifted area of his ministry.[18] He replaced Norman Shepherd's position at Westminster Seminary in Philadelphia in 1985. He was not trained under John Murray and other Old Westminster theologians like Norman Shepherd, Richard Gaffin and John Frame. Rather, he was

---

view of justification itself is a function of his view of one's vital union with Christ. As important as justification by imputed righteousness is for him, it is not justification by faith but union with Christ that is the controlling principle of the Reformer's doctrine of applied soteriology." Ibid., 379-80. It is quite interesting to observe that on the one hand Carpenter's criticism is sympathetic to the exponents of New Perspective on Paul in light of radically reinterpreted concept of union with Christ like Gaffin. On the other hand, he uses it to provide an unfair critique of the Reformed theologians' understanding of the *ordo salutis*: "Nevertheless, a couple of broad conclusions can be drawn from the foregoing. On the one hand, Calvin's understanding of justification as a function of one's union with Christ may have anticipated in some respects certain features in Paul that NT scholarship is presently highlighting.... And though Calvin is more 'ecclesiocentric' than some are willing to recognize, he does not speak of salvation as corporate or covenantal in the same way that scholars such as Hays, Wright, Dunn, and Sanders do.

On the other hand, it is not clear that Calvin's view is entirely in line with that brand of Protestant soteriology whose characteristic mark, A. A. Hodge notes, 'is the principle that the change of relation to the law signalized by the term justification...necessarily precedes and renders possible the real moral change of character signalized by the terms regeneration and sanctification.' The question may then be raised: to what extent does appealing to Calvin promote a rapprochement between Protestants and Roman Catholics? Although Calvin certainly believes that justification precedes any sustained moral improvement by the believer (progressive sanctification) the way he coordinates regeneration, the formation of and exercise of faith, union with Christ, and justification as a particular benefit of this union leads one to doubt that, if he were alive today, he would level his polemic against Roman Catholic soteriology on the precise sequence of salvation's renovative and juridical aspects in the believer.... Just as he did in his own day, I suspect that Calvin would spend more energy challenging Rome's view of sin and depravity, on the one hand, and of union with Christ, on the other, always underscoring the controlling significance of this union for every saving benefit, including justification by faith." Ibid., 385-86.

[18] I sat several times during morning devotion at Van Til Hall at Westminster Seminary in Philadelphia in my graduate study years (1993-1998) when Ferguson delivered his powerful messages. I was marveled by his passionate and powerful sermons. I think that he is one of the best Reformed preachers I have ever heard. In a word, he is a gifted preacher. I have wondered why such a gifted Reformed preacher has to reject the evangelical distinction between Law and Gospel. I have no answer for that.

trained at Aberdeen under the powerhouse of the Torrancian School in Scotland. Nevertheless, his doctoral dissertation under the supervision of James Torrance suggests that he already thoroughly understood John Murray's biblico-systematic theology, although his main topic was to deal with the theology of the great English Puritan pastor and theologian John Owen.[19] He has never directly supported Norman Shepherd's new theology as his colleague Gaffin. Rather, he provided a short critique to Norman Shepherd's view on covenant and evangelism in 1977 when he was serving the *Banner of Truth* as an editor.[20]

Unfortunately, his later writing and teaching career, including his doctoral dissertation, suggest that Ferguson has not been able to remove himself from monocovenantalism—a category in which Shepherd and several of the Westminster Seminary in Philadelphia scholars fall into. Ferguson contributed a very important article on "John Murray" in *Handbook of Evangelical Theologians*. In a sense, it is a landmark article because he mistakenly argues that Murray did not maintain the distinction between Law and Grace in his biblico-systematic theology:

> Adhering to a characteristically Reformed view of God's covenant, Murray sees a Decalogue as essentially built on God's original design for creation. The commandments are expressed negatively because they are set in the context of human depravity. Furthermore, Murray argues in detail that Old Testament and New Testament, grace and law, law and love, cannot be regarded as antithetical. In Scripture they are complimentary and indeed essential to one another. A study of the creation ordinances is therefore foundational to a proper understanding of the Christian ethic.[21]

Ferguson fundamentally misread Murray's biblico-systematic theology. It is true that Murray conceives that there is continuity between Old and

---

[19] Cf. Sinclair B. Ferguson, "The Doctrine of the Christian Life in the Theology of Dr. John Owen [1613-83]: Chaplain to Oliver Cromwell and Sometime Vice Chancellor of the University of Oxford" (Ph.D. diss., University of Aberdeen, 1979).

[20] Sinclair B. Ferguson, Review of *The New Testament Student and Theology*, ed. by J.H. Skilton. *The Banner of Truth Magazine* (July/August, 1977), 59-63.

[21] Sinclair B. Ferguson, "John Murray," in 'Handbook of Evangelical Theologians,' ed. Elwell (Grand Rapids, Michigan: Baker Book House, 1993), 179-180.

New Covenants in light of redemptive historical continuity where all the believers after the fall must be saved by the grace of God through faith alone in Jesus Christ. However, Murray does not confound law and grace in his soteriology as Ferguson misrepresented. In Murray's soteriology, he clearly maintains the distinction between Law and Gospel in respect to justification by faith alone (*sola fide*) while law becomes the positive means in the process of sanctification for those who are already justified.

We face another problem with Ferguson's analysis on Murray's biblico-systematic theology. He presents Murray as though he was a member of the Union with Christ School scholars like Gaffin, Shepherd and others. Interestingly, Ferguson interprets Murray's understanding on justification and sanctification only in light of union with Christ and eschatology, without referring to the distinction between Law and Gospel as Gaffin, who promoted it extensively in his own Pauline soteriology, did:

> We have already noted that, in Murray's view, union with Christ is 'the central truth of the whole doctrine of salvation.' In union with Christ not only do we enter into the grace of justification through his obedience (Rom. 5), but we simultaneously participate in sanctification (Rom. 6). In contrast to both Lutheran theology and popular evangelicalism, where justification dominates and sanctification serves as a codicil confirming or advancing its reality, for Murray justification and sanctification are inseparably linked to one another because both are the effect of union with Christ. Indeed, when we recognize that they are different dimensions of the Christian's existence (technically, justification is an act of God in our behalf, sanctification a work of God upon our lives), we may say that justification and sanctification begin simultaneously, both being part of the one eschatological reality of our union with Christ.
>
> Here again Murray captured and echoed Calvin's finest emphases.[22]

Thus, Ferguson mistakenly locates Murray and Calvin as if they exclusively emphasized the union with Christ in their exposition of the Pauline soteriology without referring to the distinction between Law and Gospel. In doing so, he laid a historical theological foundation to justify

---

[22] Ibid., 177-178.

rejection to the distinction between Law and Gospel for himself, the Union with Christ School scholars, and their followers.

In 1996, Ferguson published his *magnum opus*, *The Holy Spirit* while he was teaching systematic theology as a professor of Westminster Seminary in Philadelphia. This work once again demonstrates that Ferguson is a prolific writer and Reformed theologian, and a man filled with a deep pastoral sensitivity. However, his book also profoundly demonstrates his attempts to elaborate on the doctrine of the Holy Spirit without referring to the distinction between Law and Gospel, exclusively emphasizing eschatology and union with Christ as promoted by his colleague Gaffin through his Pauline soteriology. In that sense, I think that Ferguson's theological ideal perfectly parallels Gaffin's "sympathetic critical method" where the distinction between Law and Gospel is rejected in the analysis of the Pauline soteriology:

> Moreover, when union with Christ is the architectonic principle for interpreting the ministry of the Spirit, the various aspects of the application of redemption retain the vital eschatological dimension (and tension) which features so largely in New Testament thought. Those who live in the Spirit, and thus participate in Christ, also live in this world, dominated as it is by the flesh. For that reason there is always an already/not yet character to the present experience of salvation. It is doubtful whether the 'chain' model could never express this fully. Its very form suggests that one link is complete in itself and thus isolated from the others; thus, for example, regeneration is viewed as coming to an end where faith begins. In the New Testament, by contrast, there remains a yet-to-be-consummated aspect to every facet of salvation.[23]

Like Gaffin, Ferguson *exclusively* emphasizes union with Christ and eschatological tension between *already but not yet* in the Pauline soteriology. He does it at the expense of the distinction between Law and Gospel, which is a vital hermeneutical tool for the doctrine of justification by faith alone (*sola fide*). In that sense, Ferguson's critique of the traditional concept of *ordo salutis* loses balance, and echoes Gaffin's critique of the traditional *ordo salutis*:

---

[23] Sinclair B. Ferguson, *The Holy Spirit: Contours of Christian Theology*, ed. Gerald Bray (Downer Grove, Illinois: InterVarsity Press, 1996), 102-103.

The chain model for the Spirit's work tends to create the impression that the inaugurated is also the fully realized. But there is an eschatological ('already / not-yet') structure to each aspect of soteriology. Regeneration is a present reality but it also awaits its consummation (Mt. 19:28). Sanctification already involves a radical, once-for-all-break with the dominion of sin (1 Cor. 6:11; Rom. 6:1-14), but it also develops progressively to its perfection (1 Thes. 5:23). Even glorification, while consummated in the future, has already in a sense begun here and now through the indwelling of the Spirit of grace and glory (2 Cor. 4:18; Rom. 8:28; 1 Pet. 4:13). And while it requires carefully guarded statement, it is also true that justification is an already accomplished and perfect reality, but awaits its consummation – in the same way in which adoption (like justification, a *legal* act in the New Testament) will enter a new stage when we receive that for which we wait eagerly yet patiently, namely ('our adoption as sons, the redemption of our bodies' (Rom. 8:23). Similarly, while believers have already been justified with irreversible finality, they will appear before the judgment seat of Christ to receive what is due to them (2 Cor. 5:10).[24]

Another important scholar who has consistently supported Shepherd's new theology at the Westminster School is apologetician and systematic theologian John Frame. He has been highly critical of those who are critical of Shepherd's new theology. His criticism culminated in his foreword to a recently published book, including articles by Shepherd and his supporters. Critically endorsing Shepherd's writings, Frame critiques Shepherd's critics as follows:

> I hope that Shepherd's more vehement critics will listen to his words in this volume…. This is clearly a Biblical, evangelical, and Reformed understanding of the gospel and nothing else. It is so plain that frankly I find it hard to credit the intelligence or spiritual perception of anyone who objects to it. I am hoping that readers will take these words seriously. There is certainly room for disagreement with his broader discussion. But no one, I think, can legitimately doubt that he has the gospel straight…. I have tried to address this controversy and others in an irenic spirit, but

---

[24] Ibid., 103.

there are times when harsh language is appropriate. Jesus was gentle with the woman of Samaria, but he was very harsh with supposed experts in religion.... At the risk of losing my reputation for peacemaking, I must here also use some harsh language with some of Shepherd's critics (including official statements of two small denominations) who have accused Shepherd of denying the gospel or of preaching 'another gospel.'

In the light of Shepherd's writing here, quite consistent with his writings elsewhere, it should be plain that such criticisms are stupid, irresponsible, and divisive. Theological professors who make such comments, in my judgment, do not have the intellectual, theological, or spiritual maturity to prepare students for gospel ministry. Similar comments can be made against pastors, writers, and web gurus who try to turn this debate into some kind of new reformation.[25]

Unfortunately, Frame loses the theological ground to interpret Shepherd's monocovenantalism because he falls into monocovenantalism himself when he rejects adoption of the distinction between Law and Gospel in his own theological system. At the conclusion of his foreword, Frame clearly rejects the distinction between Law and Gospel, endorsing theonomic monocovenantalism after the pattern of Bahnsen:

Wagner argues that gospel and law can be understood as complementary, not antithetic, within the covenant context. I strongly agree with this thesis, and with that of Jeffrey Ventrella, who presents some vitally important principles for engaging in theological controversy. I strongly exhort readers to read Ventrella's essay before reading anything else in this book. May God use this volume to turn readers from ugly dogmatism toward a calm, gentle, and thoughtful dialogue on these important matters.[26]

---

[25] Sandlin ed., *Backbone of the Bible: Covenant in Contemporary Perspective* (Nacogdoches, TX: Covenant Media Press, 2004), xi-xii. The above quotation demonstrates that Frame is a very honest scholar, who expresses his thought and emotion fully, regardless of the reader's opinion. He is the most respected Reformed theologian among those scholars of whose feet I have had the privilege of studying, regardless of my criticism here of his support to Shepherd's new theology and monocovenantalism. However, I am highly disappointed about his understanding of historical theology and his attitude in response to his critics.

[26] Ibid., xiii.

In fact, Bahnsen, as one of the leading theonomists, supported Shepherd's new theology. He wrote his Master of Theology thesis *The Theonomic Responsibility of the Civil Magistrate* in 1973 at Westminster Seminary in Philadelphia under the supervision of Shepherd. He published it under the title *Theonomy in Christian Ethics* in 1977 with some modifications. Surprisingly, his theonomic ethics is based upon monocovenantalism, whereby he rejects any distinction between Law and Gospel. I argue that Bahnsen's monocovenantal writing actually predates Shepherd's monocovenantalism at the Westminster School in written form.[27] He openly defended Shepherd's monocovenantalism and new theology. However, like other supporters at the Westminster School, he failed to make a theological distinction between Murray and Shepherd: "But then again John Murray retires at Westminster and you have a man [Shepherd] who was very competent who took his place and because he was so competent and wrote in a way that didn't favor mass, well, the opinion of many in positions of influence, he was moved out of his position."[28]

Peter Lillback's role in the shaping and adaptation of the hermeneutics and theology of the Union with Christ School at Westminster Seminary in Philadelphia also deserves a special attention. He is a historical theologian, passionate preacher and pastor, and influential church leader. Having a dispensational theological background, he wrote a very important Ph.D. dissertation at Westminster Seminary in Philadelphia in 1985. I think that his dissertation is the culmination of Reformed monocovenantalism rejecting the antithesis between Law and Gospel in redemptive history (*historia salutis*) and the order of salvation (*ordo salutis*). As with Shepherd and the other Union with Christ School advocates, Lillback has also incorrectly injected Reformed monocovenantalism into Calvin's covenant theology.[29]

---

[27] Bahnsen's monocovenantal theonomic ethics are well expounded in his book, *Theonomy in Christian Ethics: Expanded Edition with Replies to Critics* (Phillipsburg, NJ: P & R Publishing Company, 1984). For a covenantal critique against Bahnsen's monocovenantal theonomic ethics, see my "Covenant Theology and Old Testament Ethics: Meredith G. Kline's Intrusion Ethics," *Kerux: A Journal of Biblical-Theological Preaching* 16/1 (2001): 3-32.

[28] Quoted from John W. Robbins, *A Companion to: The Current Justification Controversy* (Uniocoi, Tennessee: The Trinity Foundation, 2003), 28.

[29] However, Lillback's Reformed monocovenantalism was not without serious theological struggle. He rightly maintained the distinction between Law and Gospel in Calvin's theology in his article, "Ursinus' Development of the Covenant of Creation: A Debt

In adopting Shepherd's interpretation of Calvin in his Ph.D. dissertation, Lillback argues that Calvin did not maintain the distinction between Law and Gospel in his soteriology, thus moving away from his previous correct position in 1981 that Calvin actually maintained the distinction between Law and Gospel just like Luther and Melanchthon. He argues that in Calvin there is no distinction between Law and Gospel because unlike Luther, he emphasized the *conditionality* of the covenant. In that fashion, Lillback rejects that justification by faith alone (*sola fide*) was a common denominator between Luther and Calvin. Injecting the Reformed monocovenantalism to Calvin's hermeneutics and theology, Lillback misinterprets Calvin's writings in massive and exhaustive manner, arguing that Calvin's view on justification lies in the middle ground between Luther and the medieval nominalists:

> Thus Calvin occupies middle ground between the merit system of the medieval Schoolmen and the law/gospel hermeneutic of the Lutheran system. Calvin was able to conjoin the concept of God's acceptance of men's works with the doctrine of justification by faith alone, by making this acceptance a subordinate righteousness to justification. Because it was subordinate, it was not contrary to justification righteousness. Calvin presents a remarkable synthesis between the old system of justification of the nominalists and the new system of justification of the Reformation. In so doing he appeals to the covenant and to the Scriptures as the basis for his position.[30]

---

to Melanchthon or Calvin?" *Westminster Theological Journal* 43 (1981): 247-88. His earlier understanding of the Reformation historical theology is, of course, against the monocovenantal thought of the Union with Christ School scholars at Westminster Seminary in Philadelphia. It would be very interesting to know what sort of reaction Shepherd and Gaffin had to Lillback's article back then, inasmuch as Shepherd was still serving the seminary as professor of systematic theology while the theological controversy was going on both there and at the Orthodox Presbyterian Church. However, in his 1985 Ph.D. dissertation he moved away from his previous correct position and adopted the historical theological position of the Union with Christ School scholars where they deny the distinction between Law and Gospel in Calvin's theology. For a critical evaluation of Lillback's dissertation and book, see Jeon, *Covenant Theology*, 248-50; Cornelis P. Venema, Review of *The Binding of God: Calvin's Role in the Development of Covenant Theology*, by Peter A. Lillback *Mid-America Journal of Theology* 13 (2002): 201-09.
[30] Lillback, *The Binding of God*, 205.

Adopting the Union with Christ School scholars' assertion that Calvin along with the Westminster Standards did not maintain the distinction between Law and Gospel, Lillback radically reinterprets the Westminster Standards from the historical theological perspective of monocovenantalism as if the Westminster Standards are a monocovenantal Confessional document, which is a grave misinterpretation. He states:

Calvin obviously failed to convince either the Lutherans or the Catholics. The Lutherans still insisted on the law/gospel distinction. The Romanists still required the doctrine of merit. But, those who emerged in the tradition of Calvin recognized the covenant context of justification. These Calvinistic distinctives were codified in the Westminster Confession of Faith, articles XI and XIV. In the second paragraph of article XI dealing with justification, one reads,

Faith, thus receiving and resting on Christ and his righteousness, is the alone instrument of justification; yet is it not alone in the person justified, but is ever accompanied with all other saving graces, and is no dead faith, but worketh by love.

That these 'other saving graces' that ever accompany justification are as a result of the simultaneous blessings of the covenant of grace is seen in article XIV, paragraph II. There one finds, 'But the principal acts of saving faith are accepting, receiving, and resting upon Christ alone for justification, sanctification, and eternal life, by virtue of the covenant of grace.'[31]

Lillback uncritically accepts and adopts the Union with Christ School Scholars' interpretation on Calvin and the Westminster Standards, rejecting the distinction between Law and Gospel in Calvin and the Westminster Standards. He undermines the critical importance of the distinction between Law and Gospel in Calvin as well as the Westminster Standards in respect to the doctrine of justification by faith alone (*sola fide*). At the same time, he undermines the crucial importance of the basic agreement between Luther, Calvin and the Westminster Standards on the issue of justification

---

[31] Ibid., 208-09.

by faith alone (*sola fide*), which was rightly interpreted and understood by the hermeneutical principle of the distinction between Law and Gospel.

Likewise, he uses the concept of the believers' covenantal union with Christ to reject the distinction between Law and Gospel in Calvin and the Westminster Standards. Inevitably, in Lillback's monocovenantal injection to Calvin and the Westminster Standards there is confusion between justification and sanctification. After all, Lillback falsely argues that believers' obedience to the law is theological evidence that there is no distinction between Law and Gospel at the Westminster Standards after the pattern of Calvin's theology:

> And finally, the *agreement* between the law and the gospel in the believer's life is also asserted in the Westminster Confession: 'Neither are the aforementioned uses of the law contrary to the grace of the gospel, but do sweetly comply with it: the Spirit of Christ subduing and enabling the will of man to do that freely and cheerfully which the will of God, revealed in the law, requireth to be done.' The covenant is a unique part of the genius of the Calvinistic system. The covenant is an organizational tool of profound importance in Calvin's soteriology as it brings together the *duplex gratium*.[32]

Of course, Calvin and the Westminster divines agreed that the Law and the Gospel are not antithetical for those who are already in Christ Jesus. The law becomes a positive means for believers' progressive sanctification while it plays out a pedagogical function in the doctrine of justification. In that way, Calvin and the Westminster divines made a careful distinction between justification and sanctification while they are embraced by the concept of the covenantal union with Christ. However, Lillback falsely argues that the law as a positive means in believers' life, as if Calvin and the Westminster Divines did not maintain the distinction between Law and Gospel in the order of salvation (the *ordo salutis*).

As such, in Lillback's analysis on Calvin and the Westminster Standards, there is no room for the distinction between Law and Gospel, which is a key hermeneutical and theological principle to articulate justification by faith alone and salvation by grace alone in the Protestant Reformation and

---

[32] Ibid., 209

Reformed theology, following the pattern of Calvin's covenant theology and soteriology.

Furthermore, Lillback makes a new synthesis between Law and Gospel. Falsely interpreting Calvin's hermeneutics and theology, he suggests that "law *in* gospel" was Calvin's hermeneutical hallmark along with Ursinus against Luther's distinction between Law and Gospel:

> Now when one turns to Calvin, assuredly, Althaus is correct in asserting that his identification of the Old Testament is 'evangelical.' This is borne out in his statement to the effect that 'the covenant made with the patriarchs is so much like ours in substance and reality that the two are actually one and the same. Yet they differ in the mode of dispensation.' But such a broad statement must be understood by Calvin's careful exposition of the difference between the law and the gospel and the letter and the spirit. Calvin is committed to the law/gospel distinction when the law is conceived in a narrow sense. Yet Calvin is careful to spell out that this law/gospel distinction is not the complete statement of the relationship of law and gospel. It is when the law is spoken of in 'the restricted sense' that it is opposite to the gospel. It is likely that Melanchthon asserts a much greater distinction than Calvin. Certainly, Luther's application of the law/gospel distinction was far more sweeping than Calvin's. The question however, is which of these two expressions of the distinction between law and gospel best fits Ursinus' *Summa Theologiae* in this light, it becomes apparent that he was working with Calvin's letter-spirit distinction rather than Luther's law/gospel distinction. Question 10 articulates the idea of law *in* gospel because the covenant of creation is the demand of the new covenant, which the reconciled to God must fulfill.[33]

Here, we observe the massive confusion and misinterpretation of historical theology in Lillback's mind. We need to be clear that Calvin's distinction between Letter and Spirit is an identical category with the distinction between Law and Gospel in relation to the doctrine of justification. From the perspective of historical theology, the distinction between the covenant of works and the covenant of grace is a covenantal

---

[33] Ibid., 281.

implication of the distinction between Law and Gospel. However, this important connection is radically reinterpreted and altered by Lillback's understanding along with the other Union with Christ School scholars at Westminster Seminary in Philadelphia.

## 2. The Union with Christ School and the New Perspective on Paul

Scholars, pastors, and seminarians who have been influenced by the Union with Christ School at Westminster Seminary in Philadelphia readily adopted the New Perspective on Paul, especially as represented by N.T. Wright. I argue here that adopting covenantal nomism as expounded by the New Perspective on Paul scholars is a logical step for those who have been influenced by the Union with Christ School, given the one common denominator between the Union with Christ School and the New Perspective on Paul: a rejection of the antithesis between Law and Gospel in the exposition of the Pauline soteriology while exclusively emphasizing the idea of union with Christ. I do not think that Shepherd and the major exponents of the Union with Christ School at Westminster Seminary in Philadelphia are ready to endorse the New Perspective on Paul publicly; however, they do share a common denominator in the rejection to the distinction between Law and Gospel in the analysis of the Pauline soteriology.[34]

---

[34] E.P. Sanders's publication of *Paul and Palestine Judaism* in 1977 revolutionized the Pauline study as a whole. Since then, many New Testament scholars and others have popularized his covenantal nomism. And many others have responded critically and some sympathetic-critically. However, it is very rare to see scholars who can penetrate the central problem of covenantal nomism, which is the rejection to the Pauline evangelical distinction between Law and Gospel. I think any criticism to the New Perspective on Paul, without penetrating the denial of the Pauline evangelical distinction between Law and Gospel may end up merely scratching the surface, without touching foundational problem of the New Perspective on Paul scholars. I hope that I may provide comprehensive and critical analysis on the New Perspective on Paul in my next book, *Covenant Theology vs. the New Perspectives on Paul.* For my brief critique to the New Perspective on Paul, including bibliography, see Jeon, *Covenant Theology*, 314-18. Here, I name a few representative works by the major New Perspective on Paul scholars. James D.G. Dunn, "The Justice of God: A Renewed Perspective on Justification by Faith," *Journal of Theological Studies* 43 (1992), 1-22; idem, "The New Perspective on Paul," *Bulletin of the John Rylands*

Surprisingly, Doug Green, an Old Testament scholar at Westminster Seminary in Philadelphia, recently published a brief but very important online article demonstrating that N.T. Wright's New Perspective on Paul is Reformational and Confessional when we view it from a sympathetic critical perspective. In doing so, he blindly accepts the misconstrued theological assertion that the Pauline soteriology may be fully interpreted by the concept of union with Christ and eschatology without referring to the antithesis between Law and Gospel, typical fashion of the Union with Christ School's hermeneutics and theology.[35]

---

*University of Manchester* 65 (1983), 95-122; E.P. Sanders, *Jesus and Judaism* (Philadelphia, PA: Fortress Press, 1985); idem, *Paul and Palestine Judaism* (Philadelphia, PA: Fortress Press, 1977); N.T. Wright, *The Climax of the Covenant: Christ and the Law in Pauline Theology* (Minneapolis, Minnesota: Fortress Press, 1991); idem, *What Saint Paul Really Said* (Grand Rapids, Michigan: Eerdmans Publishing Company, 1997).

[35] Shepherd and other Union with Christ School scholars at Westminster Seminary in Philadelphia not only opened a door to the New Perspective on Paul as we see in the examples of Green and others, but also opened a door to the theology of Rome. Having been influenced by the Union with Christ School scholars as a student of the seminary, Robert A. Sungenis is representative example of those who returned to Rome from the Protestant Reformed theology. Sungenis grew up in the Roman Catholic Church, and he later converted to the Protestant Reformed faith. Unfortunately he witnessed the Shepherd Controversy while he was a student at Westminster Seminary in Philadelphia. He learned to reject the distinction between Law and Gospel in Calvin's theology from his seminary teachers, and extended it to the theology of Luther. He falsely argues that there is no distinction between Law and Gospel in Luther as well as Calvin. However, Sungenis does not grasp that the forensic or legal understanding of justification 'by faith alone' was closely tied to the hermeneutical principle of the distinction between Law and Gospel both in Luther and Calvin. Sungenis clearly fails to make a distinction between the Protestant Reformation consensus on the doctrine of justification by faith alone and Shepherd's and his supporters' view of justification by faith and obedience due to the rejection to the antithesis between Law and Gospel: "Such noted theologians as Greg Bahnsen, Gary North, and R.J. Rushdoony disputed bitterly with anti-theonomists such as Robert Godfrey, Meredith Kline, and most of the staff of Westminster Seminary, each side writing books over a period of fifteen years condemning the other's views. It is no surprise that Reformed theologian Andrew Sandlin critiques Gary North's views on justification by seeing tendencies in North's writings "a la Shepherd" of "a process contingent on human activity." North makes such wide-ranging statements as, "We are continually in God's court of law. As we work out our salvation with fear and trembling, God continually brings judgment on our activities... God continually evaluates our actions, and He declares us progressively righteous, as we mature as spiritually regenerated creatures" (Sandlin, *The Chalcedon Report*, p. 26). This is one of the first times a Reformed

Evangelical theologian has coupled forensic imputation with progressive justification, and is thus a precedent setting idea in Reformed thought. We have already seen the seed's North's view in Luther's amalgamation of the forensic and the progressive aspects of justification, as well as Calvin's merging of the judgment at "God's throne" with the "graciousness" and "acceptance" of man by God. What North fails to see, however, is that, strictly speaking, God cannot evaluate us from the perspective of law, since law must, by its very nature, condemn us for the slightest fault. Only when we understand that God views our faith and works within the realm of grace – a grace that seeks to please God *personally* not *judicially* – can there be any gratuity given to man or righteousness deemed to him. This is the Catholic view." Robert A. Sungenis, *Not by Faith Alone: The Biblical Evidence for the Catholic Doctrine of Justification* (Santa Barbara, CA: Queenship Publishing Company, 1997), 591.

The most fundamental problem in Sungenis's analysis on the Protestant Reformation understanding of the doctrine of justification lies in that he does not interpret the doctrine in light of the distinction between Law and Gospel, the hermeneutical and theological divide between Rome and the Protestant Reformation. That is the reason why he sees continuity rather than radical discontinuity between Rome and the Protestant Reformation in respect to the doctrine of justification by faith. Here, we see the hermeneutical and theological influence on Sungenis's mind of the Union with Christ School scholars' rejection of the distinction between Law and Gospel. Sungenis rightly connects Gaffin's interpretation of Pauline soteriology and eschatology with Shepherd's new theology. However, he fails to make a distinction between Gaffin and Geerhardus Vos. To be sure, Vos's Pauline eschatology never undermined the doctrine of justification by faith alone in light of the Pauline antithesis between Law and Gospel along with the distinction between the covenant of works and covenant of grace: "Other Reformed theologians say almost the same thing as Shepherd but without following their reasoning to its logical conclusion. For example, R. C. Sproul writes, 'All who are regenerated are changed… Faith is the fruit of regeneration… The necessity, inevitability, and immediacy of good works are linked to the work of regeneration' (*Justification by Faith Alone*, ed. John Armstrong, p. 26). Hence, we ask: if faith and good works are the fruit of regeneration, then how can faith be separated from good works in justification? Perhaps Luther anticipated this contradiction and thus insisted, in opposition to Calvin, on faith preceding regeneration. Interestingly, one of Shepherd's original supporters at Westminster, Professor of New Testament Richard Gaffin, wrote a book in 1978 (around the time the Shepherd controversy was brewing) titled the *Centrality of Resurrection*, which was republished under the title *Resurrection and Redemption: A Study in Paul's Soteriology*, in 1987. In the book, Gaffin argues that Reformed theology's entire concept of the *ordo salutis* is a misapplication of Paul's thought. Gaffin draws support for his thesis from two prominent figures of the Reformed faith, Geerhardus Vos (*The Pauline Eschatology*, 1930); and Hermann Ridderbos (*Paul: An Outline of His Theology*, 1966, 1975). In place of the *ordo salutis*, Gaffin proposes that Paul's soteriology is essentially eschatological with specific reference to the resurrection of Christ, and to the believer's union with him both spiritually and physically as the unifying theme of the New Testament. Gaffin points out the failure of the traditional *ordo salutis* in several respects." Ibid., 592-93.

Green's article is very important because it echoes the opinions of some of the professors who are sympathetic to the expounders of the New Perspective on Paul, especially N.T. Wright at Westminster Seminary in Philadelphia:

> Recently, frustration has been expressed at the failure of certain professors at Westminster Theological Seminary (PA) to express publicly their sympathy for the New Perspective in general and Tom Wright in particular. While I cannot speak for any of my colleagues, I will speak for myself.
>
> There are many reasons for my silence. For one, I recognize that as a professor at Westminster, I need to speak responsibly and circumspectly when commenting on or taking sides in theological debates. Additionally, there is the problem of the 'political' climate. When respected Reformed theologians describe Wright's views as 'dangerous' and 'an attack on the very heart of the gospel' and more extreme voices denounce 'Wright's Antichristian theology,' it is hardly an environment that encourages seminary professors – let alone those who teach at Westminster – to stand up and say, 'Hold on, maybe Wright's on to something here. Let's be a little less suspicious and see what we can learn.'[36]

To be sure, Vos emphasized the Pauline eschatology in light of the life, death and resurrection of Christ. However, his Pauline eschatology makes a beautiful harmony, affirming justification by 'faith alone' (*sola fide*) in light of the antithesis between Law and Gospel while he interprets the doctrine of justification, including all the soteriological blessings in the comprehensive concept of the union with Christ. That is the reason why I argue that there is fundamental difference between Vos and Gaffin. See Geerhardus Vos, *The Pauline Eschatology* (Phillipsburg, NJ: P&R Publishing Company, 1994); Jeon, *Covenant Theology*, 79-94.

Unfortunately, there are some theologians, pastors, and seminarians among Vosians, who exclusively emphasize the Pauline eschatology, without reckoning the distinction between Law and Gospel in the analysis of the order of salvation and redemptive history. Put simply, they have lost balance, and will have a devastating impact to the Church and its followers.

Scott Hahn has taken a very similar road like Sungenis. He was a former Protestant and returned to Rome after he was heavily influenced by the Union with Christ School scholars. Since then, he has promoted Roman Catholic theology. See Scott Hahn & Kimberly, *Rome Sweet Home* (San Francisco, CA: Ignatius, 1993).

[36] Doug Green, "N.T. Wright – A Westminster Seminary Perspective," (http://www.ntwrightpage.com/Green_Westminster_Seminary_Perspective.pdf).

Green argues that his positive endorsement of *The New Perspective on Paul* should not be controversial because it is in harmony with redemptive historical hermeneutics and theology as expounded and promoted by Westminster Seminary in Philadelphia:

> Some words of explanation are in order. These comments should not be particularly controversial, especially for those who embrace a redemptive-historical approach to Scripture. You won't find any stunning new insights. I say nothing here that hasn't already been said many times on this list. Finally, these remarks will make most sense when read in the context of the hermeneutical and theological distinctives of Westminster Theological Seminary (PA).[37]

In his brief assessment on N.T. Wright's *New Perspective on Paul,* Green makes seven points of "What I Like" and five points of what he terms "Possible Weaknesses." I think that as an Old Testament scholar, his approach is well-balanced and careful in that respect. Nevertheless, his evaluation is fundamentally flawed because he evaluates N.T. Wright's covenantal nomism through the lenses of the Union with Christ School scholars' redemptive historical hermeneutics and theology, exclusively emphasizing the concept of union with Christ along with eschatology, without reckoning the antithesis between Law and Gospel. So, it is necessary to dissect Green's positive remarks on it, as he writes in his paper:

> (2) *Wright's hermeneutical stance is strongly redemptive-historical / covenantal and Christocentric (or 'Christotelic').* Wright places the story of Christ – his life, death, resurrection, heavenly reign and return – at the center of Paul's gospel. This is consistent with Westminster Seminary's approach both to biblical hermeneutics and systematic theology.
>
> (3) More specifically, *Wright takes 'the Israelness' of redemptive (or, covenantal) history very seriously* – more seriously, I think, than does the tradition launched by the Westminster Standards. Consequently, for Wright, *the Old Testament plays an important role in understanding*

---

[37] Ibid.

*Paul's soteriology.* It is at this point that Wright significantly improves on our tradition.

(4) Wright has a *good understanding of the deeply eschatological character of Paul's gospel* – something that redemptive-historical exegetes from the Reformed tradition have also emphasized….

(6) I fundamentally agree with the analysis that sees *Wright's approach to Paul as compatible with Calvin's emphasis on union with Christ.* At Westminster Seminary, union with Christ – rather than justification by faith – is viewed as the organizing center of Pauline soteriology. This emphasis – along with the tradition of redemptive-historical hermeneutics and the consequent subordination of *ordo salutis* to *historia salutis* in soteriology – *should* encourage a sympathetic reading of Wright, at least in those strands of Confessional Reformed theology are more indebted to Calvin than to Luther.

(7) Wright's reading of Paul coheres well with the message of the Gospels – especially when they are read in terms of the Kingdom of God rather than forced to fit a justification-centered gospel.[38]

Green's positive evaluation on Wright's *New Perspective on Paul* heavily relies upon Gaffin's Reformed monocovenantal concept of union with Christ, eschatology, and the Pauline soteriology, interpreted without the implication of the antithesis between Law and Gospel. Moreover, Green's historical implication about Calvin and the Westminster Standards in relation to N.T. Wright is based upon the Union with Christ School scholars' understanding of historical theology, which is fundamentally flawed.[39] It is true that Gaffin's concept of union with Christ, eschatology,

---

[38] Ibid.

[39] Green uncritically accepts Gaffin's interpretation on Calvin and the Westminster Standards from a monocovenantal perspective where he rejects the distinction between Law and Gospel in the analysis of justification by faith and the Pauline soteriology. Furthermore, he uncritically accepts Rich Lusk's inpterpretation on N.T. Wright's concept of the Pauline eschatology, which is fundamentally flawed. Ibid.

Gaffin thoroughly reinterprets 'the order of salvation' (the *ordo salutis*) in Calvin and the Westminster Standards in light of the Reformed monocovenantalism of the Union with Christ School whereas the concept of union with Christ is exclusively emphasized in the depiction of soteriology. It is the reason why Green's understanding of historical theology and identification of Reformed theology is at best so confused because he heavily relies on Gaffin's lead on this regard. See Richard B. Gaffin Jr., "Biblical Theology and

and justification is by and large critically harmonious with N.T. Wright because both reject the Pauline antithesis between Law and Gospel in relation to justification by faith. It seems that Green does not grasp the fundamental problem of N.T Wright's redemptive historical hermeneutics and theology based upon the rejection of the Protestant Reformation principle of the antithesis between Law and Gospel, a principle that was a key hermeneutical principle to interpret justification by faith alone against the medieval Schoolmen's legalism. In addition, Green does not understand that justification by faith alone in light of the antithesis between Law and Gospel was a Protestant Reformation consensus between Luther and Calvin. In this respect, I am deeply puzzled by Green's assertion that Wright's concept of union with Christ is fundamentally compatible to Calvin's view. To be sure, Calvin never jeopardized the antithesis between Law and Gospel in his exposition of justification by faith alone although he beautifully embraces all the soteriological blessings under the umbrella of the concept of union with Christ, including justification and sanctification.

It is lamentable that Green as an Old Testament scholar at Westminster Seminary in Philadelphia does not read monocovenantalism either in Wright's concept of union with Christ or in Gaffin's. In his analysis on Wright's "possible weaknesses," Green argues that Wright needs to adopt the centrality of union with Christ in his Pauline soteriology after the pattern of Gaffin's Pauline soteriology:

> (5) While Wright's work is quite compatible with Paul's emphasis on union with Christ, in my opinion he has *not (as yet) done justice to the centrality of this doctrine.* This is a point at which Wright could perhaps benefit from interaction with those in the conservative Reformed tradition who have done most to develop this doctrine.[40]

---

the Westminster Standards," in *The Practical Calvinist: An Introduction to the Presbyterian and Reformed Heritage: In Honor of D. Clair Davis' Thirty Years at Westminster Theological Seminary*, ed. Peter A. Lillback (Great Britain: Christian Focus Publication, 2002), 425-42. Gaffin's same article was republished later with a minor modification, see idem, "Biblical Theology and the Westminster Standards," *Westminster Theological Journal* 65 (2003): 165-79.

[40] Green, "N.T. Wright – A Westminster Seminary Perspective." However, Green is not the first scholar who fell into New Perspective on Paul after he was influenced by

I wholeheartedly agree with Green that N.T. Wright is a thought–provoking Pauline scholar, prolific writer, and enlightening thinker. Yet, his critical endorsement in light of the theologies of Calvin and the Westminster Standards is absolutely misleading. For an example, Green does not recognize that N.T. Wright follows E.P. Sanders's basic premise that the Protestant Reformation misread Paul, denying the antithesis between Law and Gospel. After the pattern of Sanders, Wright attacks the heart of the Reformation understanding of Paul. Wright rejects the adoption of the Reformation understanding of justification by faith alone and the gospel, and radically and thoroughly reinterprets them from the principle of covenantal nomism, which rejects the distinction between Law and Gospel along with the distinction between the second and third uses of the law:

> Many people, including many supposedly 'Pauline Christians,' would say, off the cuff, that the heart of Paul's teaching is 'justification by faith.' What many such people understand as the meaning of this phrase is

---

the Union with Christ School scholars. Before Green, Don B. Garlington is a notable Pauline scholar, who adopted the New Perspective on Paul after he was influenced by the Union with Christ School as Green recognizes it in his footnotes 21 & 22: "21 While identifying himself as a New Perspective theologian and sympathetic to Wright, Don Garlington, "A Study of Justification," *Reformation & Revival Journal* 11:2 (Spring 2002) 55-73 (67), makes a similar point: "[Wright's] overall treatment of justification is rendered less than adequate because it does not allow for a righteousness that finds is very origin in the believer's union with Christ." I note with interest that Garlington is a graduate of Westminster Seminary (M.Div. 1973; Th.M. 1975). I suspect that both his appreciation for and his criticism of Wright at some level have their origins in his seminary training.

22 It is understandable but a little unfortunate that Wright appears to be unfamiliar with Gaffin's work in this area." Ibid.

In relation to Green's confusion, it is worth mentioning Nicholas Perrin's review article, "A Reformed Perspective on the New Perspective." Perrin in his critical review manifests that he is at best a confused Pauline scholar. Especially, his identification between Murray and Wright on the concept of "mystical union with Christ" is simply false and disastrous. Indeed, Murray's biblico-systematic theology has nothing to do with Wright's radically redefined concept of the union with Christ and is a million miles away from Wright's New Perspective on Paul. See Nicholas Perrin, "A Reformed Perspective on the New Perspective," Review of *Justification and the New Perspective on Paul: A Review and Response* (2004), by Guy Prentiss Waters *Westminster Theological Journal* 67 (2005): 381-89.

something like this. People are always trying to pull themselves up by their own moral bootstraps. They try to save themselves by their own efforts; to make themselves good enough for God, or for heaven. This doesn't work; one can only be saved by the sheer unmerited grace of God, appropriated not by good works but by faith. This account of justification owes a good deal both to the controversy between Pelagius and Augustine in the early fifth century and to that between Erasmus and Luther in the early sixteenth century.

In the present chapter I shall suggest that this popular view of 'justification by faith,' though not entirely misleading, does not do justice to the richness and precision of Paul's doctrine, and indeed distorts it at various points. I shall then suggest a more appropriate way of connecting Paul's 'gospel,' which we discussed in chapter 3, and the full Pauline meaning of 'justification.' Briefly and baldly put, if you start with the popular view of justification, you may actually lose sight of the heart of the Pauline gospel; whereas if you start with the Pauline gospel itself you will get justification in all its glory thrown in as well.[41]

As such, at the heart of N.T. Wright's redemptive historical hermeneutics and theology, he denies the antithesis between Law and Gospel along with the antithesis between obedience and faith. For that reason, I argue that his *New Perspective on Paul* is anti-Reformational and anti-Pauline. Ultimately, it is indistinguishable between justification and sanctification in Wright's covenantal nomism as Norman Shepherd's and the Union with Christ School scholars' monocovenantalism where the distinction between Law and Gospel is rejected. Wright in his discussion on the Pauline justification and holiness appears to refute at the same time Pelagian moralism and anti-moralism or antinomianism. However, he does so by collapsing and confusing faith and obedience, which is an Achilles heel of *The New Perspective on Paul* scholars and their followers and sympathizers:

But this is a travesty. Paul's doctrine of justification is completely dependent upon his gospel, which as we have seen is the proclamation

---

[41] N.T. Wright, *What Saint Paul Really Said: Was Paul of Tarsus the Real Founder of Christianity* (Grand Rapids, Michigan: Eerdmans Publishing Company, 1997), 113.

of Jesus as Lord. Allegiance to this Jesus must be total. *One of Paul's phrases is 'the obedience of faith.' Faith and obedience are not antithetical. They belong exactly together. Indeed, very often the word 'faith' itself could properly translated as 'faithfulness,' which makes the point just as well.* [Emphasis added] Nor, of course, does this then compromise the gospel or justification, smuggling in 'works' by a back door. That would only be the case if the realignment I have been arguing for throughout were not grasped. Faith, even in this active sense, is never and in no way a qualification, provided from the human side, either for getting into God's family or for staying there once in. It is the God-given badge of membership, neither more or less. Holiness is the appropriate human condition for those who, by grace alone, find themselves as believing members of the family of God.[42]

So in Wright's understanding of the Pauline soteriology, the believer's soteric blessings, such as justification and sanctification, are indistinguishable. Here, Wright advances in a more radical way. He puts the Pauline doctrine of justification not into the category of soteriology but ecclesiology. I think that it is one of the primary reasons the major exponents of the Union with Christ School are not ready to endorse Wright's view on covenant and justification by faith, unlike Green and others in Westminster Seminary in Philadelphia and beyond:

I have, of course, foreshortened discussion of these difficult and contentious matters a great deal. But already it should be clear that certain aspects of the post-Augustine debate of what has come to be called 'justification' have nothing much to do with the context in which Paul was writing. 'Justification' in the first century was not about how someone might establish a relationship with God. It was about God's eschatological definition, both future and present, of who was, in fact, a member of his people. In Sanders' terms, it was not so much about 'getting in,' or indeed about 'staying in,' as about 'how you could tell who was in.' In standard Christian theological language, it wasn't so much about soteriology as about ecclesiology; not so much about salvation as about the church.[43]

---

[42] Ibid., 160.
[43] Ibid., 119.

It is obvious at this point that the Union with Christ School scholars and Wright's *New Perspective on Paul* have a common consensus in their rejection of the distinction between Law and Gospel although they have a different approach and theological motivation to do so. But there is tension between the major exponents of the Union with Christ School and some of their followers based upon whether they accept or reject *The New Perspective on Paul*.

In conclusion, Green, from the perspective of the Reformed monocovenantalism as represented by the Union with Christ School, especially Gaffin, falsely argues that Wright does not deny the principle of the gospel, and that his redemptive historical hermeneutics and theology are harmonious with the Reformed understanding of redemptive historical hermeneutics and theology, including the Westminster Standards:

> Some of Wright's conservative Reformed critics have hinted that there are many positive aspects to Wright's interpretation of Paul, but they have nonetheless chosen to focus on the problem areas. I adopt a different stance, choosing to emphasize the positive contribution and placing the problem areas in the background. I do this because I am confident that Wright has not denied the gospel, as some appear to be claiming. Furthermore, as one who locates himself in the redemptive-historical tradition of Reformed theology, I am of the opinion that Wright's work marks a significant advance in theological reflection on Paul. At the very least, I believe that a judicious appreciation and appropriation of much of Wright's theology is consistent with a commitment to the Westminster Standards, when interpreted from a redemptive historical and union-with Christ perspective. Putting it more optimistically, I believe that Wright's work has the potential to contribute considerably to the enrichment and development of the redemptive-historical strand of Confessional Reformed theology.[44]

---

[44] Green, "N.T. Wright – A Westminster Seminary Perspective." It is true that Gaffin as a leading exponent of the Union with Christ School is critical of the New Perspective on Paul. However, I argue that his criticism is just a surface sketch, without touching on the New Perspective's denial of the Pauline evangelical distinction between Law and Gospel. That is the reason why I argue Gaffin's Pauline soteriology and Wright's New Perspective on Paul is sympathetic-critically harmonious. For Gaffin's sympathetic-critical analysis on Wright's New Perspective on Paul, see Richard B. Gaffin Jr., "Review Essay: Paul the Theologian," *Westminster Theological Journal* 62 (2000): 121-41.

Green's public and positive endorsement of Wright's *New Perspective on Paul* as an Old Testament professor at Westminster Seminary in Philadelphia is a reflection of a very important contemporary theological movement within the Reformed and evangelical circles. It demonstrates that the Union with Christ School in Westminster Seminary in Philadelphia and the New Perspective on Paul are critically harmonious, although the roots of their theology are vastly different. They agree on the rejection of the antithesis between Law and Gospel in the Pauline soteriology and redemptive history.

## 3. The Union with Christ School and the Auburn Avenue Theology

Recently, the proponents of *The Auburn Avenue Theology* or *Federal Vision*[45] have shown their new theological voice in evangelicalism and in the Reformed churches. It is evident that they have been heavily influenced by Shepherd's and his supporters' new theology and monocovenantalism.

---

[45] *The Auburn Avenue Theology* or *Federal Vision* is a growing theological and practical movement within conservative Reformed and evangelical circles in North America. The representative exponents of this new theological movement include John Barach, Peter J. Leithart, Rich Lusk, Steve M. Schlissel, Tom Trouwborst, Steve Wilkins, Douglas Wilson, James Jordan, and others. The official inauguration of the Auburn Avenue Theology began in 2002 at the 2002 Auburn Avenue Pastors' Conference at Auburn Avenue Presbyterian Church (Presbyterian Church in America) in Monroe, Louisiana where Steve Wilkins has been serving the church as a senior pastor since 1989. For the debate between the pro Auburn Avenue Theology and the con, see E. Calvin Beisner, ed., *The Auburn Avenue Theology, Pros and Con: Debating the Federal Vision* (Fort Lauderdale, FL: Knox Theological Seminary, 2004). For more comprehensive reading on the Auburn Avenue Theology, see Steve Wilkins and Duane Garner eds., *The Federal Vision* (Monroe, Louisiana: Athanasius Press, 2004); Douglas Wilson, *'Reformed' Is Not Enough* (ID: Canon Press, 2002).

I think that by and large the proponents of the Auburn Avenue Theology are confused theologians and pastors under the heavy influence of the Union with Christ School and the New Perspective on Paul. There are many critical articles against the Auburn Avenue Theology. It is beyond the scope of my present book to interact with them. However, I think that the foundational problem of the Auburn Avenue Theology is the rejection to the evangelical distinction between Law and Gospel in hermeneutics and theology. Unfortunately, I think that many scholars and pastors who are critically responding against the Auburn Avenue Theology are not aware of this central problem.

More precisely, the Auburn Avenue Theology is a product of a combination of the Union with Christ School's monocovenantalism and covenantal nomism as represented by E. P Sanders, N. T. Wright, and others. People may wonder why, on the one hand, the proponents of the Auburn Avenue Theology support Shepherd and the other Union with Christ School scholars, and on the other hand, N. T. Wright's covenantal nomism. It is because Shepherd and the other Union with Christ School scholars and covenantal nomism share a monocovenantalist viewpoint in which both reject the distinction between Law and Gospel in their theological system, although the root of the two theologies is very different. For example, Rich Lusk as one of the proponents of the Auburn Avenue Theology, uncritically adopts the Union with Christ School's misreading of historical theology that Calvin did not maintain the distinction between Law and Gospel in his theological system:

> Calvin paid lip service to Luther's law/gospel antithesis, but it never became a controlling feature of his theology (and certainly not of his exegesis) as it was for Luther. In fact, Calvin took a much more positive view of the law's role in redemptive history. According to Calvin the law does indeed show up sin, but that is accidental to its real purpose, which is to serve as a moral guide.
>
> The law/gospel antithesis simply doesn't work as a hermeneutic for a number of reasons. We will focus on two, first showing that law and gospel actually perform the same (rather than contradictory) functions, and then showing that they are simply two phases in the same redemptive program.[46]

---

[46] Beisner ed., *The Auburn Avenue Theology*, 131. In his rejection of the evangelical distinction between Law and Gospel in Calvin's theology, Lusk follows and adopts Frame's rejection to the distinction between Law and Gospel, which is disastrous. That is a major reason why I argue that the major exponents of the Auburn Avenue Theology at best are confused theologians and pastors. So, I think a starting point of hermeneutical and theological problems of the Auburn Avenue Theology lies in their rejection of the distinction between Law and Gospel in Leviticus 18:5. Lusk also follows exactly the unfortunate footsteps of Frame and Jordan's monocovenantalism: "A fuller analysis of the law/gospel contrast is provided by John Frame.... I cannot deal in this essay with every possible text. For a survey of how some key NT texts, often appealed to as law/gospel proof texts, should be read covenantally, consult James Jordan "Thoughts on the Covenant of Works (Part 2)".... Jordan gives special attention to the troublesome

Rich Lusk and other proponents of the Auburn Avenue Theology, like Shepherd and the other Union with Christ School scholars, identify their monocovenantalism with Calvin's theology. Moreover, Lusk with other Auburn Avenue Theology promoters, adopt covenantal nomism, as represented by the New Perspective on Paul scholars:

> To the extent that Reformed Protestantism has individualized the message of salvation, and to the extent that N.T. Wright, J.D.G. Dunn, and others call us back to a corporate view of salvation, it does indeed look like a 'different gospel' is being proclaimed. But these 'different gospels' are not really at odds, any more than eggs and omelets are at odds (to steal another of Wilson's illustrations). Wright's view gives the gospel a broader sweep (since he makes it clear the corporate includes the individual), but compared to our truncated version of the gospel it looks *really* different. The problem is our myopia. We've looked at the gospel from about two inches away for four centuries, and our long-distance vision is dysfunctional. Wright and others, meanwhile, are asking us to look at the gospel from 30,000 feet up. Or, to use an alternative illustration that Peter Leithart has used in his Eucharistic studies, we have gotten used to looking at the gospel through a narrow zoom lens; the 'New Perspective' gives us the wide angle view. Sure, it looks different, but that's to be expected. The 'New Perspective' never denies that Paul actually taught what Luther and Calvin claimed–namely, *sola gratia* and *sola fide*.[47]

Here Lusk evidences the degree to which he has been misdirected about historical theology in respect to the Protestant Reformation in the sixteenth century. He does not understand that justification by faith alone

---

use of Leviticus 18:5 in the New Testament. My only caveat is to suggest that Leviticus 18:5 is not referring to "earning" eternal life through doing the things of the law; rather the "life" envisioned is life in the land of promise. So long as Israel lives out the Torah (which could only be done by faith, at root), she could continue under God's favor and would enjoy the full realization of the blessings God intended for her in the Mosaic economy. But the law as such belonged to the old age and could not bring forth the eschatological order. The life graciously promised in exchange for Torah observance is still pre-eschatological." Ibid.

[47] Ibid., 135-36.

and salvation by grace alone are closely related to the antithesis between Law and Gospel both in Luther and Calvin. He does not know that if anyone rejects the antithesis between Law and Gospel, any affirmation of *sola gratia* and *sola fide* is a mere lip service and a self-contradiction.

Like Shepherd and his supporters at the Union with Christ School, Lusk and other promoters of Federal Vision or Auburn Avenue Theology fundamentally misread the Protestant Reformation. The most foundational problem is that they do not recognize the antithesis between Law and Gospel in Calvin's soteriology and Pauline soteriology. In other words, they read Calvin's theology and the Bible from a radical monocovenantal perspective. In addition, they fail to see that the basic thesis of covenantal nomism, as represented by the New Perspective on Paul scholars, is to reject the distinction between Law and Gospel in the analysis of the Pauline soteriology and theology just as Barth's existential monocovenantalism does.[48]

The influence of the Union with School scholars at Westminster Seminary in Philadelphia, including Shepherd, on the Auburn Avenue Theology is very significant. They reject the distinction between Law and Gospel in Calvin's theology after the pattern of the Union with Christ School scholars. Moreover, they interpret justification by faith only in respect to union with Christ, without referring to the distinction between Law and Gospel. For example, Lusk argues that Calvin's views on "imputation and forensic justification" may be fully interpreted through the exclusive concept of union with Christ. Furthermore, he identifies Calvin's view on justification by faith in Christ with a contemporary Reformed theologian, Gaffin. Again, Lusk fails to understand Calvin's understanding on justification by faith alone, which is closely related, on the one hand, to the concept of union with Christ, and on the other hand, to the distinction between Law and Gospel:

Calvin situates imputation and forensic justification in the broader context of union with Christ.

A similar pattern of theologizing is found in more contemporary Reformed theologies. For example, Richard B. Gaffin argues:

---

[48] For a covenantal critique against covenantal nomism, see Jeon, *Covenant Theology*, 314-18.

'Paul does not view the justification of the sinner (the imputation of Christ's righteousness) as an act having a discrete structure of its own. Rather, as with Christ's resurrection, the act of being raised with Christ in its constitutive, transforming character is at the same time judicially declarative; that is, the act of being joined to Christ is conceived of imputatively. In this sense the enlivening action of resurrection (incorporation) is itself a forensically constitutive declaration.'

Gaffin affirms the forensic nature of justification, but roots it in union with Christ. Imputation, as such, has no free standing structure of its own. It is simply a corollary of union with Christ. We may conceive of union with Christ imputatively, if we wish, but the key is to affirm that if we are *in Christ* we share in his right standing before the Father (cf. 1 Corinthians 1:30).[49]

Likewise, Lusk is a representative example that the exponents of the Auburn Avenue Theology interpret Calvin's doctrine of justification by faith exclusively in reference to the concept of union with Christ, without the antithesis between Law and Gospel, because they see this important hermeneutical and theological tool as Luther's unique idea. As a result, they make Calvin to be a monocovenantalist, as if he rejected justification by faith alone. In doing so, they identify Gaffin's eschatological monocovenantalism with Calvin's soteriology, even though the two are fundamentally incompatible. Lusk's interpretation on Calvin's justification by faith as exclusively emphasizing the concept of the union with Christ without referring to the distinction between Law and Gospel, reveals that the foundational problem of the Auburn Avenue Theology, following the footsteps of the Union with Christ School, finds its origins in the influence of the Union with Christ School scholars. Now, we fully realize the hermeneutical and theological problem we face when we reject the distinction between Law and Gospel. In fact, the five points of Calvinism has been systematically destroyed and altered in the theological minds of the Auburn Avenue Theology promoters.

---

[49] Beisner, ed., *The Auburn Avenue Theology*, 143.

Thus, monocovenantalism, in rejecting the antithesis between Law and Gospel in the analysis of justification by faith at the Westminster School is not just a monopoly of Norman Shepherd. It has grown progressively amongst some prominent scholars ever since Murray's retirement in 1966. It has merged and spread to Bahnsen's monocovenantal theonomic ethics, his followers, the followers of the Union with Christ School, and the proponents of the theology of Federal Vision, among others.

## C. Rejection of the Antithesis between the Covenant of Works and the Covenant of Grace

The development of 'the covenant of works' (the *foedus operum*) in respect to the prelapsarian Adamic paradise has been the distinctive hallmark of Reformed theology developed after Calvin. Of course, Calvin did not use the word 'covenant' (*foedus*) for the prelapsarian Adamic status. However, Calvin did lay out all the biblical theological ingredients toward the development of the covenant of works among Calvinists in the latter part of the sixteenth century. It was sharpened and flowered in Puritan theology in the seventeenth century. And the theological substance of the distinction between the covenant of works and the covenant of grace was beautifully laid out in the Westminster Standards (1643-1648).[50]

It is very important to note that the antithesis between the covenant of works and the covenant of grace is a covenantal implication of the distinction between Law and Gospel, which was a crucial hermeneutical tool for Calvin's theology. Karl Barth and his followers vehemently rejected the distinction between the covenant of works and the covenant of grace, which has been a comprehensive and profound hermeneutical tool for Reformed theology. Therefore, it is logical for them to be critical of the

---

[50] The followers of Karl Barth's existential monocovenantalism rejecting the antithesis between the covenant of works and the covenant of grace along with the distinction between Law and Gospel have provided a serious critique of the Calvinist's development of the antithesis between the covenant of works and covenant of grace, including the Westminster Standards. So, they have argued "Calvin against the Calvinists" in respect to the historical development of federal theology. For the Barthian critique against the development of federal theology, see Jeon, *Covenant Theology*, 11-14.

Confessional adaptation of the distinction between the covenant of works and the covenant of grace.

Shepherd, following Berkouwer, plainly rejects the covenant of works. In that sense, he is consistent in his monocovenantalism in his rejection of the covenant of works:

> Moses, the mediator of the old covenant, wrote Genesis as an introduction to this covenant. He wrote to explain where human beings came from, how sin entered into human experience, and why the plan of redemption takes the form of a covenant. In the beginning God created the heavens and the earth. *He created the first man and the first woman in his own image unlike the animals—so that he could fellowship with them in union and communion. They were created as his covenant partners with the promise of life to be received by faith. In the command not to eat of the Tree of Knowledge, it was the faith of Adam that was being tested.* [Emphasis added] The issue was whether he would live by every word that comes from the mouth of the Lord. Adam believed Satan instead of God, and from this unbelief flowed the disobedience that plunged him and the whole human race he represented into sin, condemnation, and death (Rom. 5:12). Because he would not forsake his original purpose in creating Adam and Eve, the Lord God undertook to redeem the human race. Redemption does not destroy creation but renews it and restores lost mankind to covenant union and communion with his Maker. The Lord unfolds the plan of redemption in a series of historical covenants beginning with Noah. The account of Noah reveals just how serious the problem of sin is (Gen. 5:6) and how destructive the consequences of sin are not only for human beings but also for the world in which they live. In the covenant with Noah God promises to preserve the world as a platform for the unfolding of the drama of redemption (Gen. 9:11), and he reassigns to the human race the original cultural mandate given to Adam (Gen. 9:13). In the covenant with Abraham God promises that there will be a redeemed human race to inhabit this preserved world (Gen. 15:5). He obligates Abraham and his descendants to covenantal faith and loyalty as the way in which he intends to bring about everything that he has promised to him (Gen. 18:17-20). Ultimately, *through the covenantal faith and loyalty of Jesus Christ who was obedient to death, even death on the cross, the promise to Abraham is fulfilled* [Emphasis added]

and the nations are discipled into the new covenant as they are marked by baptism (Gal. 3:16).[51]

It is quite interesting to observe Shepherd's description of the prelapsarian Adamic condition. Unlike his predecessor John Murray, Shepherd recognizes its covenantal character. However, he plainly denies the substance of the Adamic covenant of works whereas Murray maintains the substance of the distinction between the covenant of works and the covenant of grace, although he was hesitant to designate "covenant" as the terminology applicable to the prelapsarian status. This is yet another reason why Shepherd's new theology is incompatible with that of Murray, his predecessor at Westminster Seminary in Philadelphia. Here, we find the distinctive nature of Shepherd's theology. He rejects the idea that Adam was standing as a representative covenant head who should have fulfilled God's covenantal demand of perfect obedience to the law in order to obtain confirmed righteousness and eschatological heavenly blessings for himself and his descendents whom he represented. Here, he departs significantly from Reformed theology as well as from Calvin. Shepherd's monocovenantalism rejects the distinction between Law and Gospel and the distinction between the covenant of works and the covenant of grace, and in the process the antithesis between Adam and Christ disappears. Shepherd argues that Adam's *faith* was the way to the promise of life while under the new covenant, the promise to Abraham was fulfilled through "*the covenantal faith and loyalty of Jesus Christ.*" In this radical new interpretation, the historical order of Law and Gospel, not vice versa, which is warranted by the Pauline antithesis, disappears.[52]

---

[51] Norman Shepherd, "My Understanding of Covenant" (www.spindleworks.com/library/CR/shepherd.htm).

[52] I argue that Murray as the predecessor of Shepherd and other Union with Christ scholars at Westminster Seminary in Philadelphia maintained *the theological and hermeneutical substance* of the distinction between the covenant of works and covenant of grace in respect to the prelapsarain Adamic status although he was hesitant to designate it as a covenant of works. Murray, over against the Union with Christ scholars, carefully maintained the historical and logical order of the Law and Gospel, not vice versa. In that sense, *Murray against the Murrayans* may be a correct historical theological analysis when we compare Murray's biblico-systematic theology with Union with Christ scholars' new theology. For a comprehensive and critical analysis on Murray's view on the distinction between the covenant of works and the covenant of grace, see Jeon, *Covenant Theology*, 103-44, 280-307.

We need to be reminded that Shepherd and his supporters have consistently argued that his theology is compatible with the Westminster Standards. However, they undermine the hermeneutical and theological foundation that the formulation of justification by faith alone in the Confession was closely related not only to the distinction between Law and Gospel, but to the distinction between the covenant of works and the covenant of grace as well. The Westminster divines were self-consciously clear that justification by faith alone stand and fall together with the antithesis between Law and Gospel. Its covenantal implication is the distinction between the covenant of works and the covenant of grace.

The Westminster divines beautifully laid out the *distinction* between the covenant of works and the covenant of grace in the Westminster Standards, whereas Shepherd clearly rejects this distinction. In the Standards, it is clearly demonstrated that eternal-heavenly life was promised by God to Adam and his posterity upon condition of "perfect and personal obedience," which was revealed in Genesis 2:17. This is rightly called "a covenant of works." After the fall, God introduced a new way of eternal-heavenly blessing, which is called "the covenant of grace," wherein, the means of justification and eschatological heavenly blessing are not "perfect and personal obedience" to the law, but rather "faith" in Jesus who fulfilled all the requirements of the covenant of works as a sinless Mediator through his life and death, paying the penalty of sins as the Confession states:

> 1. The distance between God and the creature is so great, that although reasonable creatures do owe obedience unto Him as their Creator, yet they could never have any fruition of Him as their blessedness and reward, but by some voluntary condescension on God's part, which He hath been pleased to express by way of covenant.

---

In that sense, I think that Ferguson's critical posture against the Confessional adaptation of the distinction between the covenant of works and the covenant of grace is fundamentally different from Murray's apparent rejection to the covenant of works. Ferguson, like other Union with Christ School scholars, rejects the historical and logical order of Law and Gospel, which is closely tied to the distinction between Law and Gospel in relation to justification by faith alone. For Ferguson's critical posture against the covenant of works, see Sinclair B. Ferguson, "The Teaching of the Confession," in *The Westminster Confession in the Church Today*, ed. Alasdair I. C. Heron (Edinburgh: The Saint Andrews Press, 1982) 28-39.

2. The first covenant made with man was a covenant of works, wherein life was promised to Adam; and in him to his posterity, *upon condition of perfect and personal obedience.* [Emphasis added]

3. Man, by his fall, having made himself incapable of life by that covenant, the Lord was pleased to make a second, commonly called the covenant of grace; wherein He freely offereth unto sinners life and salvation by Jesus Christ; *requiring of them faith in Him,* [Emphasis added] that they may be saved, and promising to give unto all those that are ordained unto eternal life His Holy Spirit, to make them willing, and able to believe.[53]

Here, we find the genius of Reformed theology, which is distinctively biblical and Pauline at the same time. The Westminster divines guarded the redemptive historical order as the covenant of works and the covenant of grace. Ultimately, the law in the prelapsarian paradise was the means of the eschatological heavenly blessings, while the gospel in Jesus was the only means of the eschatological heavenly blessings in the postlapsarian world until the Second Coming of Jesus. The Confession safeguards the historical and logical order of Law and Gospel, not vice versa. The antithesis between the covenant of works and the covenant of grace is warranted in Paul's theology. Paul made a clear distinction between Adam and Christ in his order of 'redemptive history' (*historia salutis*) and the 'order of salvation' (*ordo salutis*) (Rom. 5:12-21; 1 Cor. 15:20-24). Moreover, Paul formulated an antithesis between "the first Adam" (*ho protos Adam*) and "the last Adam" (*ho eschatos Adam*) (1 Cor. 15:45-49). The covenantal implication of the contrast of the two Adams is the absolute distinction between the covenant of works and the covenant of grace as the means of eschatological justification and heavenly blessings. Likewise, the Confessional distinction is concretely biblical and Pauline.

---

[53] The Westminster Confession of Faith, 7.1-3. I defended the distinction between the covenant of works and the covenant of grace applied in the Westminster Standards against the Barthian existential monocovenantalism and other forms of monocovenantalism. In addition, I argued that the Confession clearly stated justification by faith alone, excluding all kinds of obedience in its doctrine. For the comprehensive analysis of the Confessional distinction between the covenant of works and the covenant of grace, see Jeon, *Covenant Theology*, 40-45.

In addition, we need to be reminded that the Westminster divines understood the distinction between the covenant of works and the covenant of grace in light of the antithesis between Law and Gospel, referring to the classical Pauline passages such as Romans 10:5 and Galatians 3:12, which set forth Paul's hermeneutical and theological implications, quoted from Leviticus 18:5: "Do this and you shall live or you shall die." It is not surprising to know that Calvin already laid a concrete hermeneutical foundation that distinguished between the covenant of works and the covenant of grace. Leviticus 18:5 is a biblical hermeneutical foundation for it. As such, Calvin's distinction between Law and Gospel is not an abstract idea to expound justification by faith alone, but rather, is based upon a concrete biblical and hermeneutical idea. Calvin, examining medieval scholastic rejection of justification by faith alone and the doctrine of the supererogatory merits of the believers argues that Leviticus 18:5 is the revelation about the principle of the law, which requires the perfect obedience to the law. Of course, it is impossible to accomplish for sinners:

> If these things are true, surely no works of ours can of themselves render us acceptable and pleasing to God; nor can even the works themselves please him, except to the extent that a man, covered by the righteousness of Christ, pleases God and obtains forgiveness of his sins. For God has not promised the reward of life for particular works but he only declares that the man who does them shall live [Lev. 18:5], leveling that well-known curse against all those who do not persevere in all things [Deut. 27:26; Gal. 3:10]. *The fiction of partial righteousness is abundantly refuted by these statements, where no other righteousness than the complete observance of the law is allowed in heaven.* [Emphasis added]
>
> Their usual loose talk about 'works of supererogation' providing sufficient compensation is no sounder. Why? Do they not always return to the position from which they have already been driven, that he who partly keeps the law is to that extent righteous by works? What no one of sound judgment will concede to them they too shamelessly assume as a fact. *The Lord often testifies that he recognizes no righteousness of works except in the perfect observance of his law.* [Emphasis added][54]

---

[54] Calvin, *Institutes*, 2.14.13.

Shepherd and the Union with Christ School scholars at Westminster Seminary in Philadelphia do not allow Leviticus 18:5 as the principle of the law, which requires the perfect obedience to the law for sinners' justification by faith alone and heavenly blessings. In that sense, they removed the biblical and hermeneutical foundation for justification by faith alone and salvation by grace alone. As such, Shepherd rejects the adoption of the Reformation hermeneutical tradition rightly developed by Calvin and adopted by the Calvinists and the Westminster Standards. In doing so, he radically reinterprets Leviticus 18:5. Certainly, in the Reformed hermeneutics and theology after the pattern of Calvin's hermeneutical and theological tradition, Leviticus 18:5 has been used as a mirror of the antithesis between Law and Gospel. When applied to soteriology, it became a reference point not for sanctification but justification. But, Shepherd's hermeneutics and theology reject this:

> The law is a gracious gift that embodies wisdom for living. "Now choose life, so that you and your children may live…. The Lord is your life" (Deut. 30:19-20). This is also the thrust of Leviticus 18:5, "Keep my decrees and laws, for the man who obeys them will live by them. I am the Lord." This verse does not challenge Israelites to earn their salvation by their good works. Rather, it offers to all who are covenantally loyal and faithful the encouragement and assurance that they will live and prosper in the land. This is the Lord's promise to them, a promise to be received with a living and active faith.[55]

To be sure, Shepherd takes a very alienated hermeneutical road, compared to Calvin and Reformed hermeneutics as a whole. Paul quotes Leviticus 18:5 in Romans 10:5 and Galatians 3:12 to use it as a hermeneutical and theological reference point that Law and Gospel or the covenant of works and the covenant of grace are absolutely antithetical in relation to justification and salvation. From that perspective, of course, Calvin, Calvinists, and the Westminster divines interpreted and adopted it. However, Shepherd denies this important hermeneutical and theological tradition:

---

[55] Shepherd, *The Call of Grace*, 36.

Before we leave this point, we need to look at two passages in which Paul appears to describe the Mosaic covenant as a covenant of works. The first is Romans 10:5-6: "Moses describes in this way the righteousness that is by the law: 'The man who does these things will live by them.' But the righteousness that is by faith says: 'Do not say in your heart, "Who will ascend into heaven?" (that is, to bring Christ down).'" *The other is Galatians 3:12, "The law is not based on faith; on the contrary, 'The man who does these things will live by them.'" Both of these passages quote Leviticus 18:5, apparently as though it establishes a works / merit principle in opposition to a faith / grace principle.* [Emphasis added][56]

Accordingly, in Shepherd's hermeneutics and theology, there is no room for justification by faith alone and salvation by grace alone, which was rightly expounded and understood during the Protestant Reformation and adopted and developed in the Reformed hermeneutics and theology.

In addition, the antithesis between the covenant of works and the covenant of grace was a logical development from Calvin's theology, where the antithesis between Adam and Christ was demonstrated. Certainly, Calvin's justification by faith alone was interpreted by the *antithesis* between Adam and Christ, based upon the Pauline construction of the two Adams:

---

[56] Ibid., 36-37. Reflecting on the Shepherd Controversy (1975-1982) on covenant and justification by faith, I wish that scholars and pastors should have focused more on the distinction between Law and Gospel in relation to justification by faith, which is the foremost foundational problem of Shepherd's and his supporters' new theology. The contemporary debate about elder John Kinnaird's view on covenant and justification by faith is just a revival of the Shepherd Controversy in similar theological issues at the Orthodox Presbyterian Church. I suggest that the participants in the debate should focus more on the Pauline evangelical distinction between Law and Gospel in the milieu of Deut. 18:5; Rom. 10:5-6; and Gal. 3:10-12, because I think that Kinnaird follows the exact footsteps of the monocovenantalism of Shepherd and other Union with Christ School scholars. In that sense, I think that the debate in the OPC in respect to Kinnaid's theological views will be the debate between monocovenantalists siding with Kinnaird on the one hand, and scholars and pastors who go against Kinnaird's views, maintaining the distinction between Law and Gospel in relation to justification by faith alone. In any case, the wide division in respect to Kinnaird's view on covenant and justification by faith in the OPC is simply a reflection that historical theological stability in the OPC as well as at Westminster Seminary in Philadelphia has been lost for the past several decades after John Murray's retirement from his teaching position in 1966. By and large, I think that this is due to the heavy influence of monocovenantalism of the Union with Christ School in that denomination.

*By his obedience, however, Christ truly acquired and merited grace for us with his Father. Many passages of Scripture surely and firmly attest this.* [Emphasis added] I take it to be a common place that if Christ made satisfaction for our sins, if he paid the penalty owed by us, if he appeased God by his obedience–in short, if as a righteous man he suffered for unrighteous men–then he acquired salvation for us by his righteousness, which is tantamount to deserving it.... The meaning therefore is: God, to whom we were hateful because of sin, was appeased by the death of his Son to become favorable toward us. *And we must diligently note the antithesis that follows thereafter.* [Emphasis added] "As by one man's disobedience many are made righteous." [Rom. 5:19.] This is the meaning: as by the sin of Adam we were estranged from God and destined to perish, so by Christ's obedience we are received into favor as righteous. The future tense of the verb does not exclude present righteousness, as is apparent from the context. For, as Paul had said previously, "the free gift following many trespasses is unto justification" [Rom. 5:16].[57]

Likewise, Shepherd's rejection of the antithesis between Adam and Christ in his theological construction is a significant departure from both the Westminster Standards and Calvin's theology. Calvin profoundly insisted that justification by faith alone is closely related to the meritorious obedience of Christ, which was understood in light of the antithesis between Adam and Christ (Rom. 5:12-21). It is important to remember that Calvin's antithesis between Adam and Christ is substantially the same as the Confessional formulation of the antithesis between the covenant of works and the covenant of grace. In that sense, it is very clear that the Westminster Standards' adaptation of the antithesis between the covenant of works and the covenant of grace is not alien to Calvin's theology.

Indeed, Calvin himself provided the hermeneutical and theological foundations of Calvinists' distinction between the covenant of works and the covenant of grace, locating Genesis 3:15 as the beginning of redemptive history, which was "the first promise of salvation" in Christ, "the Sun of Righteousness":

---

[57] Calvin, *Institutes*, 2.17.3.

Coming down to the later prophets, we can walk freely, as it were, in our own field. For, if we proved our point without difficulty as far as David, Job, and Samuel were concerned, in the Prophets it is much easier. The Lord held to this orderly plan in administering *the covenant of his mercy* [Emphasis added]: as the day of full revelation approached with the passing of time, the more he increased each day the brightness of its manifestation. Accordingly, at the beginning when the first promise of salvation was given to Adam [Gen. 3:15] it glowed like a feeble spark. Then, as it was added to, the light grew in fullness, breaking forth increasingly and shedding its radiance more widely. At last—when all the clouds were dispersed—Christ, the Sun of Righteousness, fully illumined the whole earth [cf. Mal., ch. 4].[58]

Likewise, Calvin was a wonderful redemptive historian. He self-consciously interpreted the Bible from the perspective of redemptive history as inaugurated in Genesis 3:15. He powerfully demonstrated the progressive nature of redemptive history, which culminated in the Coming of Jesus, "the Sun of Righteousness." However, his redemptive historical understanding never denied justification by faith alone and salvation by grace alone in his soteriology. That is a reason why his theology has a profound balance, a balance shattered in the theology of Shepherd and his supporters.

Having traced Calvin's theological suitability to the Calvinist's development of the distinction between the covenant of works and the covenant of grace, it is worth exploring Lillback's understanding of Calvin's role in the latter Calvinists' development of the covenant of works.[59]

Lillback argues that Calvin embraced an "inchoate covenant of works" although he did not use the term, "covenant of works." According to Lillback, Calvin's hermeneutics and theology are compatible to the Calvinists' distinction between the covenant of works and the covenant of grace. So far, so good, but at the heart of Lillback's analysis of Calvin's covenant theology, he substantially misreads and distorts Calvin because he denies the distinction between Law and Gospel in relation to the distinction between the covenant of works and the covenant of grace.

---

[58] Ibid., 2.10.20.
[59] Lillback, *The Binding of God*, 276-304.

On the surface, Lillback appears to adopt Muller's famous thesis of "Calvin and the Calvinists" against the Barthian "Calvin against the Calvinists" in respect to the development of the covenant of works:

> Finally, in chapter 15 it has been argued that Calvin reveals an inchoate prefall covenant that can with qualifications be demonstrated a covenant of works. This is in the spirit of the "Muller-Thesis" that seeks to recognize substantial continuity and organic development between the Reformers and Protestant Scholasticism. Here we challenge McGiffert, Rolston, Torrance, and Bruggink, who pit the Federalists against Calvin. We also find unconvincing the views of Althaus, Barth, Lang, Ritschl, Schrenk, and Sturm who credit Melanchthonian influence on Reformed theology for the emergence of the prelapsarian covenant. There is significant agreement between Ursinus' first expression of the covenant of creation and Calvin's own idea of the letter-spirit distinction. Even though Calvin failed to interpret all of the typical federalist texts in a federalist fashion, this did not stop him from speaking of a covenant with Adam in the garden with the sacrament of the tree of life. Moreover, Calvin's idea of Adam in a probationary period, under the duty of obedience to law, with life as the benefit, anticipates the federal arrangement. Calvin unites the moral law with the law of God written on men's consciences.[60]

It is so important to note that in Calvin, the distinctions between Law and Gospel and Letter and Spirit are coterminous. But, Lillback denies this vitally important fact because he denies reading the distinction between Law and Gospel in Calvin as the other Union with Christ School scholars, including Shepherd, have falsely argued. Here, once again, we need to notice that the distinction between the covenant of works and the covenant of grace is simply a covenantal and redemptive historical implication of the distinction between Law and Gospel. In that sense, Lillback's apparent affirmation of Calvin's "inchoate covenant of works" is self-contradictory, and he adds not clarification but more confusion to his readers and followers.

---

[60] Ibid., 310-11.

Shepherd likewise denies the distinction between the covenant of works and the covenant of grace as carefully adopted in the Westminster Standards. His rejection to any distinction between these two covenants is logical and consistent with his monocovenantalism, where he rejects the distinction between Law and Gospel. Lillback, however, appears to affirm "the inchoate covenant of works" in his analysis on Calvin's covenant theology. I argue that Lillback's apparent affirmation of the covenant of works in respect to the prelapsarian Adamic status in Calvin's theology is misreading and false because he rejects and does not connect it to the distinction between Law and Gospel found in Calvin. This linkage of the covenant of works and Law and Gospel distinction is foundational for the later Calvinists' distinction between the covenant of works and the covenant of grace. Perhaps Lillback undermines or ignores the crucial importance of the hermeneutical and theological presupposition of the distinction between Law and Gospel in the development of the distinction between the covenant of works and the covenant of grace. In a word, the affirmation of the distinction between covenant of works and covenant of grace without affirming and relating this distinction to the distinction between Law and Gospel is self-contradictory and mere lip service. It is another reason why the followers of the Union with Christ School scholars are so misled and confused.

# II.
## Justification by Faith

Shepherd's monocovenantalism, which rejects the antithesis between Law and Gospel along with the distinction between the covenant of works and the covenant of grace, directly influenced his radical reinterpretation of covenant and justification by faith. He consciously reinterpreted the classical Protestant doctrine of justification by faith alone in light of his monocovenantalism. Thus, it is necessary to interact comprehensively and critically with his radical reinterpretation of justification by faith and with other closely related hermeneutical and theological issues. In doing so, it is also necessary to address the views of Shepherd's supporters and other closely related theologians.

## A. Rejection of the Imputation of the Active Obedience of Christ

During the seven years of theological controversy at the Westminster Seminary and the Philadelphia Presbytery of the Orthodox Presbyterian Church (1975-1982), Shepherd never denied *explicitly* the doctrine of the imputation of the active obedience of Christ. However, it is my contention that he had already denied it *implicitly*. For example, Shepherd presented a paper entitled, *The Relation of Good Works to Justification in the Westminster*

*Standards* on October 1 and 2, 1976, to defend his theological formulation among faculty members. In this paper, he thoroughly reinterpreted the doctrine of covenant and justification by faith, reinterpreting the Westminster Standards in light of his monocovenantalism. I would argue that his implicit rejection of the doctrine of the imputation of the active obedience of Christ is logically consistent with his monocovenantalism, where he rejects the distinction between Law and Gospel and the distinction between the covenant of works and the covenant of grace.

Interestingly, Shepherd explicitly does deny the doctrine of the imputation of the active obedience of Christ in his recent writings, *Backbone of the Bible* in 2004 with the title, "Justification by Works in Reformed Theology." Again, he finds his primary theological reasoning in his rejection of the imputation of the active obedience of Christ, appealing to historical theology and the lack of the biblical evidence, as he did in his rejection of the antithesis between Law and Gospel. He argues that he does not find the concept of the imputation of the active obedience of Christ in earlier Reformed theology such as that of Calvin, Ursinus or the Heidelberg Catechism. He insists that the concept of the active obedience of Christ is a theological innovation of the later Reformed scholastics in the seventeenth century, which then merged into the Reformed theological tradition:

> We do not find a belief in the imputation of active obedience in Calvin, Ursinus, or the Heidelberg Catechism for the reason that their understanding of justification as the remission of sins did not require it and they did not find it in the Bible. The very few Bible texts quoted by later theologians in support of this doctrine are understood by earlier theologians to refer to the imputation of the righteousness Christ wrought out in his suffering and death for his people in obedience to the will of his heavenly father. Even the Westminster Confession as late as 1647 was written as a compromise document to accommodate the views of three prominent members of the Westminster Assembly (William Twisse [Prolocutor of the Assembly], Thomas Gataker, and Richard Vines) who did not subscribe to the imputation of active obedience.[1]

---

[1] Shepherd, "Justification by Works in Reformed Theology," 115.

However, this is another misreading and distortion of historical theology. It is true that there is no room for the imputation of the active obedience of Christ in Shepherd's monocovenantalism. My major criticism of Shepherd is not his rejection of the imputation of the active obedience of Christ. Rather, it is his distortion of historical theology. He reinterprets the earlier Reformed theology in light of his own radical monocovenantalism. But his historical theological misreading is absolutely disastrous not only to his own theological formulation but to that of his followers as well. He does not understand that Calvin's and Ursinus's distinction between Law and Gospel in relation to justification by faith alone and salvation by grace alone already implicitly embraces the concept of active obedience. The Reformed Scholastics' distinction between the active and passive obedience of Christ is simply an unpacking of the perfect obedience of Christ to the requirement of the law in light of the antithesis between Law and Gospel, which Calvin, Ursinus, and the Heidelberg Catechism applied and adopted. My point is that the doctrine of the active obedience of Christ and the antithesis between Law and Gospel stand and fall together. Shepherd falsely argues that there is no theological evidence for the concept of the imputation of the active obedience of Christ in the earlier Reformed theology or in the Bible:

> However we do find confessional language that has been interpreted as affirming the imputation of active obedience. For example, in Lord's Day 23 of the Heidelberg Catechism we have, as already noted, references to the satisfaction, righteousness, and holiness of our Lord being imputed to sinners for their justification. But interpreting these as a reference to the imputation of active obedience is a reading back into earlier Reformed theology of views that developed only at a later time. Early Reformed theology had no doctrine of the active obedience because it defined soteric justification as the forgiveness of sins. Justification meant that God forgives our sins and on that basis accepts us as righteous and gives us the title to eternal life. There is no imputation of active obedience because the faith/grace paradigm within which they understood justification did not require it and no Bible texts taught it.[2]

---

[2] Ibid., 115.

In spite of Shepherd's above assertion, we must understand that Calvin unambiguously taught that there are two aspects of spiritual blessings in the idea of justification by faith alone. One is the forgiveness of sins, and the other is the clothing with Christ's righteousness in light of the perfect obedience to the law through his life and death. Shepherd does not acknowledge that God's clothing act with Christ's righteousness is coterminous with the imputation of the active obedience of Christ:

> If we are to determine a price for works according to their worth, we say that they are unworthy to come before God's sight; that man, accordingly, has no works in which to glory before God; that hence, stripped of all help from works, he is justified by faith alone. But we define justification as follows: the sinner, received into communion with Christ, is reconciled to God by his grace, while cleansed by Christ's blood, *he obtains forgiveness of sins, and clothed with Christ's righteousness as if it were his own, he stands confident before the heavenly judgment seat.* [Emphasis added][3]

Shepherd tries to abandon from Protestant theology the important concept of the imputation of righteousness of Christ in the forensic act of God's declaration of justification in Paul, Calvin and earlier Reformed theology. He incorrectly argues that justification is "simply the forgiveness of sin," exclusively emphasizing the death and resurrection of Christ while deleting the importance of his perfect life in the arena of justification:

> My point in taking up Ursinus and the Heidelberg Catechism is simply to demonstrate that in the early phase of the Reformation our Reformed theologians accurately reflected the teaching of Paul. I could have demonstrated the same point from Calvin and other early confessions. Justification is simply the forgiveness of sin grounded in the death and resurrection of Christ. This fact explains the concurrence between Luther and Calvin on the doctrine of justification.[4]

---

[3] Calvin, *Institutes*, 3.17.8.
[4] Shepherd, "Justification by Works in Reformed Theology," 111.

However, Calvin clearly proclaimed that justification by works and justification by faith are antithetical in respect to God's sight. In other words, man may be "justified by faith or works," but there is no amalgam between works and faith in the concept of justification. He clearly argued that justification lies in the forgiveness of sins *and* the imputation of Christ's righteousness, earned through his perfect obedience in respect to the requirement of the law in his life and death:

> Thus, justified before God is the man who, freed from the company of sinners, has God to witness and affirm his righteousness. In the same way, therefore, he in whose life that purity and holiness will be found which deserves a testimony of righteousness before God's throne will be said to be justified by works, or else he who, by the wholeness of his works, can meet and satisfy God's judgment. On the contrary, justified by faith is he who, excluded from the righteousness of works, grasps the righteousness of Christ through faith, and clothed in it, appears, in God's sight not as a sinner but as a righteous man.
>
> *Therefore, we explain justification simply as the acceptance with which God receives us into his favor as righteous men. And we say that it consists in the remission of sins and the imputation of Christ's righteousness.* [Emphasis added][5]

Shepherd's historical theological understanding and description are simply a reflection of the great confusion of his historical theological mind. This is another indication that his historical theological reading is not compatible with Murray. Murray would never argue that there is no active obedience of Christ in Calvin's theology. To be sure, Calvin did not use the words, active and passive obedience of Christ. However, the two aspects of Christ's meritorious obedience through the course of his entire life are unambiguously manifested in Calvin's writings and thought. Calvin beautifully describes the two aspects of Christ's perfect obedience as follows:

> Now someone asks, How has Christ abolished sin, banished the separation between us and God, and acquired righteousness to render

---

[5] Calvin, *Institutes*, 3.11.2.

God favorable and kindly toward us? To this we can in general reply that he has achieved this for us by the whole course of his obedience. This is proved by Paul's testimony: "As by one man's disobedience many were made sinners, so by one man's obedience we are made righteous" [Rom. 5:19 p.]. In another passage, to be sure Paul extends the oasis of the pardon that frees us from the curse of the law to the whole life of Christ: "But when the fullness of time came, God sent forth his Son, born of woman, subject to the law, to redeem those who were under the law" [Gal. 4:4-5]. Thus in his baptism, also, he asserted that he fulfilled a part of righteousness in obediently carrying out his Father's commandment [Matt. 3:15]. In short, from the time when he took on the form of a servant, he began to pay the price of liberation in order to redeem us.

Yet to define the way of salvation more exactly, Scripture ascribes this as peculiar and proper to Christ's death. He declares that "Christ died for our sins" [Rom. 4:25.]. John the Baptist proclaimed that he came "to take away the sins of the world," for he was "the Lamb of God" [John 1:29 p]. In another passage Paul teaches that "we are freely justified through the redemption which is in Christ, because he was put forward as a reconciler in his blood" [Rom. 3:24-25 p.]. Likewise: "We are...justified by his blood ... and reconciled ... through his death." [II Cor. 5:21].[6]

Calvin never ignored the meritorious obedience of Christ in his depiction of salvation and justification by faith alone as Shepherd did. Calvin persuasively argued that there is neither forgiveness of sins nor the imputation of the infinite righteousness of God without Christ's perfect obedience through the entire course of his life from incarnation to death. Calvin maintained and embraced the active and passive obedience of Christ without naming it as such. Calvin further commented upon Christ's perfect obedience throughout his life and death as follows:

For this reason the so-called "Apostles' Creed" passes at once in the best order from the birth of Christ to his death and resurrection, wherein the whole of perfect salvation consists. Yet the remainder of the obedience

---

[6] Ibid., 2.16.5.

that he manifested in his life is not excluded. Paul embraces it all from beginning to end: "He emptied himself, taking the form of a servant,... and was obedient to the Father unto death, even death on a cross" [Phil. 2:7-8 p.]. And truly, even in death itself his willing obedience is the important thing because a sacrifice not offered voluntarily would not have furthered righteousness. Therefore, when the Lord testified that he "laid down his life for his sheep" [John 10:15 p.], he aptly added, "No one takes it from me" [John 10:18].[7]

Certainly, the Westminster Standards do not mention the two aspects of the Mediator's perfect obedience through his entire life unto death. However, just like Calvin, the Confession laid out the substance of the active and passive obedience of Christ. In short, the Confession did not rob Christ of his active obedience as Shepherd does. The Confession describes the two aspects of the Mediator's perfect obedience to the requirement of the law as follows:

> This office the Lord Jesus did most willingly undertake; which that He might discharge, he was made under the law, and did perfectly fulfill it; endured most grievous torments immediately in His soul, and most sufferings in His body; was crucified, and died, was buried, and remained under the power of death, yet saw no corruption. On the third day He rose from the dead, with the same body in which He suffered, with which also He ascended into heaven, and there sitteth at the right hand of His Father, making intercession, and shall return, to judge men and angels, at the end of the world.[8]

Shepherd likewise misreads and distorts early Reformed theology, mistakenly arguing that there is no concept of the imputation of the active obedience of Christ in its texts, including those of Calvin.

Interestingly, Frame, as a consistent supporter of Shepherd's new theology, disagrees with Shepherd on the issue of the active obedience of Christ. Mentioning John Piper's affirmation of it, he argues that it

---

[7] Ibid.
[8] The Westminster Confession of Faith, 8.4.

is biblical doctrine, although he also acknowledges there is room for disagreement.

It is a well-known fact that Piper used to be the most famous disciple of Daniel Fuller's hermeneutics and theology. Fuller's hermeneutics is based upon the rejection of the Reformation hermeneutical principle of the antithesis between Law and Gospel. Fuller's hermeneutics can be identified as *the obedience of faith hermeneutics*, in contrast to the Reformation principle of the distinction between Law and Gospel. Fuller rejects the distinction between Law and Gospel, following the lead of Karl Barth. However, Fuller's rejection of the distinction between Law and Gospel is much less confusing than that of the Union with Christ School scholars, including Shepherd, because Fuller recognizes that the distinction between Law and Gospel is the Reformation principle seen in both Luther and Calvin as well as the latter Reformed covenant theologians.

What I argue is that Fuller's analysis of historical theology in respect to the distinction between Law and Gospel is a correct assessment, even though he refuses to adopt it in his hermeneutics and theology. The following statement may be the most important hermeneutical and theological statement ever penned by Daniel Fuller:

> I realized that if the law is, indeed, a law of faith, enjoining only the obedience of faith and the works that proceed there from (I Thess. 1:3; II Thess. 1:11), then there could no longer be any antithesis in biblical theology between the law and the gospel. I then had to accept the drastic conclusion that the antithesis between law and gospel established by Luther, Calvin, and the covenant theologians could no longer stand up under the scrutiny of biblical theology.[9]

As a faithful and representative disciple of Fuller's obedience of faith hermeneutics that reject the distinction between Law and Gospel, Piper has popularized this approach in his writings, teaching, and preaching. Needless to say, there has been no room for justification by faith alone, the imputation of the active obedience of Christ, and the distinction between

---

[9] Daniel P. Fuller, *Gospel and Law: Contrast or Continuum?: The Hermeneutics of Dispensationalism and Covenant Theology* (Grand Rapids, Michigan: Eerdmans Publishing Company, 1980), xi.

justification and sanctification in Fuller's and Piper's obedience of faith hermeneutics and theology.

Recently, however, Piper has shown positive signs of having moved away from his former hero Fuller's hermeneutics and theology. Welcoming his hermeneutical and theological break from his former teacher, no less than 22 famous Reformed and evangelical theologians and pastors endorse his book, *Counted Righteous in Christ* with laudatory comments and praise. For that reason alone, his book demonstrates its impact and importance in respect to the contemporary debate on justification by faith and the imputation of Christ's righteousness in a sinner's forensic justification.[10]

Clearly, although he agrees with Shepherd's rejection to the distinction between Law and Gospel, Frame disagrees with Shepherd on the issue of the imputation of the righteousness of Christ or the active obedience of Christ, mentioning Piper's recent analysis:

> Nor am I ready to abandon the doctrine of the imputation of Christ's active obedience (2). There is room for debate as to whether the New Testament teaches this doctrine explicitly. John Piper has recently made a strong case that it does. But we should also look at the implications of Jesus' sacrifice, affirmed by Shepherd in theses (3) and (4). Shepherd affirms that justification is God's forgiveness, based on Jesus' death and resurrection. But, it may be argued, that forgiveness *implies* an imputation of active righteousness as well. Hebrews 9:14 and 1 Peter 1:19 describes Jesus in Old Testament sacrificial terms as without spot or blemish, doubtless referring to his sinless life. Jesus' perfect sacrifice implies and presupposes his sinless life. Now remember that Jesus is our *substitute.* Jesus who is perfectly righteous substitutes himself for us sinners. God accepts his *person*, and us in him. So it is not only Jesus' moment of death that is credited or imputed to us; it is the whole Christ, living and dying. It seems to me that one element of this imputation is that of his active obedience.[11]

---

[10] John Piper, *Counted Righteous in Christ: Should We Abandon the Imputation of Christ's Righteousness* (Wheaton, Illinois: Crossway Books, 2002).

[11] Sandlin ed., *Backbone of the Bible*, x. For a comprehensive and critical analysis of John Piper's obedience of faith hermeneutics and theology along with Daniel Fuller's, see my book, *Covenant Theology*, 143-144, 253-256, 264-270. It seems that Frame does a mere lip service in affirming the doctrine of imputation of active obedience of Christ when he does not recognize the distinction between Law and Gospel, which is implied *sine qua non* by the doctrine of imputation of Christ's active obedience.

However, Frame's apparent affirmation of the imputation of the active obedience of Christ while rejecting the classical Pauline distinction between Law and Gospel in the analysis of justification and salvation is inconsistent and confusing. He is, in fact, simply self-contradictory.

Interestingly, Frame in his endorsement of Piper's most famous book parallels Piper's *Counted Righteous in Christ* with John Murray's defense on the issue of the imputation of Christ's righteousness: "This is certainly the most solid defense of the imputed righteousness of Christ since the work of John Murray fifty years ago. I'm delighted that Dr. Piper has established that important doctrine, not as a mere article from the confessional tradition, but on the solid foundation of God's Word."[12]

One must deeply admire Piper's effort to maintain the active obedience of Christ and the imputation of the righteousness of Christ in believer's justification over against the contemporary rejection of it by Robert Gundry and the exponents of the New Perspective on Paul, including his former hermeneutical and theological model, Daniel Fuller. At one level, I can endorse his book so highly. However, as a former critic of his obedience of faith hermeneutics, I am not ready to endorse his book as much as others. In particular, I think that Frame's identification of Piper with Murray does not do justice to Murray's biblico-systematic theology. To be sure, Murray's discussion on justification by faith alone, affirming the distinction between the active and passive obedience of Christ and the imputation of the righteousness of Christ, has a hermeneutical and theological foundation, namely the distinction between Law and Gospel along with the concept of union with Christ. However, Piper does not address the foremost important issue, which is the distinction between Law and Gospel. I think that without the implication of the antithesis between Law and Gospel, any affirmation of the active obedience and the imputation of Christ's righteousness in believers' forensic justification is mere lip service. In other words, the distinction between Law and Gospel is a hermeneutical and theological foundation for the active obedience of Christ and the imputation of Christ's righteousness.[13]

As a leading exponent of the Union with School scholars, Gaffin is very similar to Frame. His eschatological monocovenantalism, exclusively

[12] Piper, *Counted Righteous in Christ*, 3. It also appears on the back cover of the book.
[13] See Jeon, *Covenant Theology*, 144–85.

emphasizing union with Christ and eschatology in the Pauline soteriology, rejects the distinction between Law and Gospel as we already observed. In that respect, there is no room for the active obedience of Christ and the imputation of Christ's righteousness in believer's forensic justification. To be sure, Gaffin agrees with Shepherd on his rejection of the distinction between Law and Gospel. However, unlike Shepherd, Gaffin argues that he affirms the active obedience of Christ and the imputation of Christ's righteousness. In his endorsement of Piper's *Counted Righteous in Christ*, Gaffin argues that indeed "the imputation of Christ's righteousness in Christ" is the Reformational doctrine and the Pauline doctrine that stands against the contemporary critique of the New Perspective on Paul scholars:

> Largely a result of the emergence in recent decades of the 'new perspective' on Paul is the growing denial today that the apostle teaches the imputation of Christ's righteousness to believers. *Counted Righteous in Christ* is such an important book because it confronts this denial head-on and counters the charge that the heart of the Reformation doctrine of justification rests on a misunderstanding of Scripture. Written in the author's typically spirited and winsome fashion, it provides what is most urgently needed in the face of this charge: a clear and convincing *exegetical* case for the gospel truth affirmed in its title. The broader church is deeply indebted to John Piper for what it has been given to him to produce in the midst of the already overly full demands of a busy pastorate.[14]

The above endorsement by Gaffin hints that Shepherd and Gaffin disagree with each other on the issue of the active obedience of Christ and the imputation of the righteousness of Christ in believer's justification, even though they belong to the same school, namely the Union with Christ School, that rejects the distinction between Law and Gospel in relation to justification by faith alone.

Frame's critical endorsement of Shepherd's new theology on the issue of the imputation of the active obedience of Christ, along with Gaffin's apparent affirmation, is a representative example that the Union with

---

[14] Piper, *Counted Righteous in Christ*, 4. It is in a front page of endorsement section.

Christ School theologians are not unified in their detailed analysis on the issues of covenant and justification by faith, although they are in complete agreement in the rejection of the antithesis between Law and Gospel, exclusively emphasizing union with Christ as a hermeneutical tool in the understanding of Pauline soteriology and Calvin's soteriology.

## B. Rejection of the Idea of Merit

In Shepherd's monocovenantalism, there is no room for the imputation of the active obedience of Christ as we have discussed. At the same time, his monocovenantalism logically rejects the meritorious obedience of Christ. Simply, there is no room in his theology for the antithesis between Adam and Christ. Thus, he rejects the distinction between the covenant of works and the covenant of grace, along with any antithesis between Law and Gospel. Therefore, it is logical to deny the idea of merit in his theological formulation. However, a bigger problem is not his rejection of the idea of merit, but his distortion of historical theology. He plainly argues that the idea of merit is not biblical. He argues that the medieval Schoolmen wrongly applied the meritorious concept to sinners' justification and salvation. In doing so, he also blames Reformed theologians who affirm the imputation of the righteousness of Christ based upon Christ's meritorious obedience through his life and death. In doing so, Shepherd incorrectly argues that Calvin did not affirm the meritorious obedience of Christ. He does not recognize that there is no fundamental difference between Calvin and the latter Reformed theology in respect to the imputation of the righteousness of Christ, which is directly related to Christ's meritorious obedience. He falsely separates the Reformation and several Reformed theologians:

> The imputation of the active obedience of Christ is absolutely essential to an evangelical view based on the works/merit paradigm. Without it, either there is no justification, or justification takes place on the ground of personal (infused and/or performed) righteousness. We are then back with Rome and have rejected the Reformation. This is why for some Reformed theologians the gospel itself stands or falls with a belief in the imputation of active obedience. From within the works/merit paradigm

justification is grounded either on the believer's own active obedience or on the active obedience of Christ imputed to him. Since the believer has no sinless active obedience of his own, he is totally dependent on the imputed active obedience of Christ. From within the works/merit paradigm to call the imputation of the active obedience of Christ into question cannot otherwise be understood than as a denial of the gospel.[15]

However, we need to know that Calvin did not reject the idea of merit. His complaint was directed at the medieval Schoolmen's concept and false implication of merit. He properly pointed out the problem of 'congruent merit and condign merit' (*meritum de congruo et meritum de condigno*), which was applied to believers' justification and salvation, and in effect denies the Mediator's meritorious obedience in place of sinners, who cannot fulfill the requirements of the law: "Finally, I say that it is of no use unless we give prior place to the doctrine that we are justified by Christ's merit alone, which is grasped through faith, but by no merits of our own works, because no men can be fit for the pursuit of holiness save those who have first imbibed this doctrine."[16]

Shepherd completely ignores the fact that the meritorious obedience of Christ and the imputation of Christ's righteousness stand and fall together in Calvin's theology. To be sure, Calvin rightly affirmed 'the works / merit paradigm' that Shepherd argues is not Reformational or biblical. At least in Calvin's theology, without the meritorious obedience of Christ, there is no justification by faith alone. For Calvin, justification by faith alone and Christ's meritorious obedience stand and fall together. Calvin's definition of merit is, in fact, very simple. He argues that perfect or sinless obedience to God's holy and righteous law is *meritorious*. That is why Calvin argues that Christ's obedience as the ultimate fulfiller of the requirement of the law as the second Adam where the first Adam failed to fulfill is meritorious obedience. Again, Calvin's concept of merit is closely related to the distinction between Law and Gospel. In other words, the concept of merit and the distinction between Law and Gospel stand and fall together in Calvin's theology.[17]

---

[15] Shepherd, "Justification by Works in Reformed Theology," 114-15.

[16] Calvin, *Institutes*, 3.16.3.

[17] For a comprehensive analysis on Calvin's view on the concept of merit, see Jeon, *Covenant Theology*, 19-20.

In fact, Calvin elegantly refuted the Schoolmen's concept of 'congruent and condign merit' (*meritum de congruo et meritum de condigno*) through 'the merit of Christ' (*meritum Christi*). He profoundly argued that without the meritorious obedience of Christ, there is no gift of salvation by God:

> The testimony commonly rendered to him is that whoever believes in him has been justified. These Sophists teach that no other benefits come from him except that the way has been opened for individuals to justify themselves... For they do not mean that by faith in Christ there comes to us the capacity either to procure righteousness or only to acquire salvation, but that both are given to us. *Therefore, as soon as you become engrafted into Christ through faith, you are made a son of God, an heir of heaven, a partaker in righteousness, a possessor of life; and (by this falsehood may be better refuted) you obtain not the opportunity to gain merit but all the merits of Christ, for they are communicated to you.* [Emphasis added][18]

It is very obvious that Shepherd's denial on the imputation of the active obedience of Christ along with the idea of merit is not based upon the theology of the Protestant Reformation. Certainly, his new theology is not in line with Calvin's theology, but with modern monocovenantalism where the meritorious obedience of Christ is clearly denied.

## C. Justification by a Penitent and Obedient Faith

We have seen that Shepherd and his supporters, identified as the Union with Christ School, are distinctive in their approach to historical theology, especially in respect to Calvin. They read Calvin from a covenantal perspective, which is thoroughly based on a monocovenantalism in which they reject the distinction between Law and Gospel. In that regard, Shepherd is very consistent in his monocovenantalism when he radically redefines justification by faith. As he identifies with Calvin in his rejection of the antithesis between Law and Gospel, he also identifies with Calvin

---

[18] Calvin, *Institutes*, 3.15.6.

in his reinterpretation of justification by faith. The weakest aspect of Shepherd's and his supporters' reading of Calvin's theology lies in that they make Calvin a covenant-legalist. Shepherd and his supporters locate Calvin between the medieval Schoolmen and Luther on the doctrine of justification by faith. It is the most important historical theological departure that they have appealed to constantly to justify their radical new interpretation. In his analysis of Galatians 5:6, Shepherd falsely separates Luther and Calvin. He argues as though Calvin was a covenant-legalist, asserting that Calvin did not affirm justification by faith alone but "by an obedient faith":

> Here we see the characteristic difference between the Reformed and the Lutheran ways of understanding the nature of justifying faith. For Calvin, justifying faith is an obedient faith. For Luther faith *becomes* an obedient faith *after it has justified.* But Luther also insists that a person "does not truly believe if works of love do not follow his faith." As though speaking through the mouth of Paul, Luther adds, "It is true that faith alone justifies, without works; but I am speaking about genuine faith, which, after it has justified, will not go to sleep but is active through love" (*Lectures on Galatians*, 30). Even for Luther, anything less than a genuine faith, a faith that is eventually active through love, cannot justify. This also qualifies how we are to understand what Luther means when he says that justification is by faith alone. Of course, both Luther and Calvin make clear that justification is in no way grounded in the obedience that invariably accompanies genuine faith.[19]

The Protestant Reformation formula, justification by faith alone, excluded any form of human works or obedience, according to both Luther and Calvin alike. Luther and Calvin interpreted justification by faith alone in light of an antithesis between works and faith when they expounded the Pauline soteriology. However, Shepherd and his supporters have rejected that interpretation. Shepherd also injects his understanding of justification by "a penitent and obedient faith" in his reinterpretation of the Westminster Standards. In doing so, he construes the Confessional understanding of justification by faith as a neo-legalistic Confession. In

---

[19] Shepherd, "Justification by Faith in Pauline Theology," 92-3.

a similar fashion, Shepherd tries to separate Luther and the Westminster Standards in their exposition of justification by faith, interpreting Romans 3:28 from the perspective of his monocovenantalism:

> In Romans 3:28 Paul says that we are justified by faith "apart from observing the law." Literally he says we are justified by faith "without the works of the law." Many would hold that "works of the law" includes everything that God commands in his word, all works of any kind, whether good, or bad, whether done in faith or in unbelief. This interpretation is reinforced by Luther's insertion of the word "alone" into the text of Romans 3:28 so that the verse reads that we are justified by faith *alone*, without the works of the law.
>
> The difficulty is that this interpretation brings Paul into conflict with himself. We could no longer say as Paul teaches and as the Reformed have always maintained, that justification is by a penitent and obedient faith because that would conflict with justification by faith alone, faith without works of the law.[20]

Here, we have to understand that Shepherd is thoroughly reinterpreting Calvin, the Westminster Standards, and Paul in light of his own monocovenantal perspective, wherein he rejects any antithesis between works and faith. He argues that there is no antithesis between works and faith in justification by faith in Calvin, the Westminster Standards, and Paul. According to Shepherd, only Luther affirmed the formula of justification by faith alone because he was a kind of antinomian, who misread Paul.

As we noted earlier, Calvin clearly maintained the distinction between Law and Gospel in his depiction of justification by faith alone. In addition, as we can see in Calvin's discussion of justification by faith alone, Calvin clearly notes that works-righteousness and faith-righteousness are antithetical. In fact, he affirmed Luther's formula, justification by faith alone, and it was not merely an empty theological slogan against the Schoolmen's concept of meritorious justification and salvation. Rather, he distinctly affirmed it, providing profound exegetical and theological argument from the Pauline text. It is important to acknowledge Calvin's

---

[20] Ibid., 94-5.

emphasis on justification by faith alone because he interpreted the Pauline doctrine in the light of absolute antithesis between works and faith, which is pervasive in the Pauline text:

> Now the reader sees how fairly the Sophists today cavil against our doctrine when we say that man is justified by faith alone [Rom. 3:28]. They dare not deny that man is justified by faith because it recurs so often in Scripture. But since the word "alone" is nowhere expressed, they do not allow this addition to be made. Is it so? But what will they reply to these words of Paul where he contends that righteousness cannot be of faith unless it be free [Rom. 4:2 ff.]? How will a free gift agree with works? With what chicaneries will they elude what he says in another passage, that God's righteousness is revealed in the gospel [Rom. 1:17]? If righteousness is revealed in the gospel, surely no mutilated or half righteousness but a full and perfect righteousness is contained there. The law therefore has no place in it. Not only by a false but by an obviously ridiculous shift they insist upon excluding this adjective. Does not he who takes everything from works firmly enough ascribe everything to faith alone? What, I pray, do these expressions mean: "His righteousness has been manifested apart from the law" [Rom 3:21 p.]; and, "Man is freely justified" [Rom. 3:24 p.]; and, "Apart from the works of the law" [Rom. 3:28]?[21]

## D. Van Til, Bavinck, and the Shepherd Controversy

During the seven year Shepherd Controversy, a most unfortunate event happened: Cornelius Van Til's support of Shepherd's new theology. Van Til retired from his teaching career at Westminster Seminary in Philadelphia in 1972. There is no theologian who provided a more acute critique of Karl Barth's existential neo-orthodox theology in the twentieth century than Van Til. His contribution to Reformed and evangelical theology is immense; he pioneered and developed presuppositional apologetics. Van Til closely read G..C. Berkouwer's adaptation of Barth's Christomonistic grace in which he rejected the distinction between Law and Gospel, and he severely

---

[21] Ibid., 3.11.19.

criticized Berkouwer's praise and adaptation of Barth's Chrsitomonistic existential grace.[22] It is my assessment that there is no theological evidence that Van Til approved and promoted monocovenantalism or rejected an antithesis between Law and Gospel, until he retired in 1972. He was a warrior who defended the gospel of grace against Barthianism and other forms of modern theology. How, then, could he support Shepherd's new theology as Reformed orthodoxy? It is simply a mystery. However, my major complaint lies not with Van Til but with Shepherd and his other supporters during the controversy. They all learned theology at the feet of Van Til. In my assessment, it is inexcusable to draw Van Til into the controversy to take their side. Van Til was misguided and misinformed by Shepherd and his supporters. There is no way that Van Til's theology would support Shepherd's monocovenantalism. Quite simply, Shepherd's new theology is incompatible with Van Til's presuppositional apologetics and theology. The only logical explanation may be that Van Til, after his retirement in 1972, radically lost the sharp theological mind he used to have. The following quotation demonstrates that at best, in his defense of Shepherd, Van Til was an old and confused theologian, who had lost his orthodox theological mind as can be seen in the following transcription of Van Til's verbal defense of Shepherd's formulation on justification by faith at the Philadelphia Presbytery of Orthodox Presbyterian Church:

> I think that when we begin with the idea of faith, we have to think first of all that the devils also believe and tremble. Now we have faith by which we need not to tremble because Christ on the cross said, "My God, my God, why hast Thou forsaken me?" so that His people might not be forsaken. It is finished! It was finished, once for all. Now that is, I think, beautifully expressed in this word of our Lord: [discussion of John 6:22ff.]
>
> When the multitudes wanted to make Him king because He had given them bread, and they thought it would be easy to have a handout, Jesus said, when they found the other side, "Rabbi, when did you get here?" Jesus said, "Truly I say to you, ye seek me not because ye see signs

---

22 For the assessment of Van Til's critique to Berkouwers's adaptation of Barth's Christomonistic grace, see Jeon, *Covenant Theology*, 301-03.

but because you ate the loaves and were filled. [VT: Now then comes the crucial point.] Do not work for food which perishes but for food which endures to eternal life which the Son of Man shall give to you, for of Him the Father even God has been sealed." They therefore said, "What shall we do, that we may work the works of God?" Jesus answered and said unto them, "This is the work of God, that ye may believe on Him Whom He hath sent."

*Here faith and works are identical. Not similar but identical. The work is faith; faith is work. We believe in Jesus Christ and in His salvation, that's why we do not tremble. He died for us, in our place, and the Scotsmen would say, "in our room and stead," for that substitutionary atonement, on the basis of which we are forensically righteous with God and are now righteous in His sight and shall inherit the kingdom of heaven in which only the righteous shall dwell.* [Emphasis added] And I'm going to ask John Frame if he will quote the Greek of this particular passage.

[Frame works through it reading both the Greek and English.]

I thank you. Well now, you see faith alone is not alone. Faith is *not* alone. Faith always has an object. The faith, your *act* of believing, is pointed *definitely* to God in Jesus Christ, and by the regeneration of the Holy Spirit, and conversion, it's all one, it's not a "janus face" [Janus-faced-JR] proposition, but it is not possible to give exhaustive statements in human words, human concepts. And that's why we have to be satisfied merely to do what the Scriptures and Confessions of Faith say that they [i.e. we] ought to do, and that then we are on the way, and I think that Norman Shepherd is certainly in the line of *direct descent* of [i.e. on the topic of] faith. Thank you. [Emphases noted are Van Til's][23]

In his defense of Shepherd's formulation of justification by faith, Van Til clearly declines to make an absolute antithesis between works and faith, but rather mixes works and faith. I believe that Van Til was absolutely confused and misguided here. I suggest that we have to separate the former Van Til from the latter Van Til. It is my assessment that Van Til's confusing

---

[23] Quoted from Robbins, *A Companion to the Current Justification Controversy*, 43-5.

mixture between works and faith in the doctrine of justification by faith is incompatible with the corpus of his writings, thought, and teaching until his retirement in 1972.

Quoting the above verbal defense by Van Til, John Robbins misleadingly argues that Van Til is the father of Shepherd's and his supporters' neo-legalism at Westminster Seminary in Philadelphia. In addition, he adds Herman Bavinck as a co-father of the New Westminster School's thought. He clearly misreads the theological affinity and connection that the New Westminster School exponents have had. I am sympathetic to Robbins's critique of Van Til because Van Til supported Shepherd's theology during the controversy regardless of his frail and aging condition. However, it is a great injustice to Bavinck's Reformed orthodoxy and profound scholarship when Robbins relates Shepherd's neo-legalism to Bavinck. Robbins misleadingly summarizes the root of Shepherd's neo-legalism as follows:

> All these streams of thought – Biblical theology, Reconstructionism, the New Perspective on Paul, Shepherdism, Roman Catholicism, Gaffin and Bavinck, Vantilianism and Neoorthodoxy – have contributed to the flood of Neolegalism in the churches. It would be incorrect to single out Norman Shepherd as the cause of our present calamity.... In order to be faithful, it must repudiate not only Neolegalism, but the matrix of irrationalism – exemplified in the books of Herman Bavinck and Cornelius Van Til – that gave it birth.[24]

There is clearly no theological controversy involving covenant or justification by faith in Van Til's writings completed before his retirement

---

[24] Robbins, *A Companion to the Current Justification Controversy*, 74-5. I think that Robbins's critique of Van Til and Bavinck focuses excessively on by the Clark-Van Til Controversy in respect to epistemology. I believe Gordon Clark and his followers, including Robbins, have misinterpreted and misunderstood Van Til's presuppositonal apologetics and epistemology. One of the key principles of Van Til's presuppositional apologetics is the distinction between the Creator and creature. I suggest them to reread Van Til's apologetics with that principle in mind. I hope that Robbins, as a leading follower of Clark, might be a bit more prudent in his criticism of Van Til and Bavinck. Others who are followers of Clark and Robbins tend not to critique Van Til based on sound scholarship, but rather by false character. This is harmful to the Church, to themselves, and to their followers.

in 1972. We see no justification controversy in Van Til's presuppositional apologetics. Shepherd and his supporters are mostly self-identified Van Tillians, yet I would argue that true Van Tillians have no theological controversy on covenant and justification by faith alone. Van Til, before his retirement from his teaching and writing career at Westminster Seminary in Philadelphia, was a great orthodox Reformed theologian, presuppositional apologetician, and biblical theologian. For example, his book, *The Great Debate Today* (1971), reflects his mature thought on his understanding of redemptive history in light of Geerhardus Vos's biblical theology. Interestingly, he defends divine redemptive history, inaugurated in Genesis 3:15, against different forms of modern theology in which biblical history and biblical truth were radically redefined by modern philosophers and theologians, as represented by Immanuel Kant, Karl Barth, and others. Unlike the Union with Christ School scholars, Van Til did not separate Luther and Calvin on the issue of justification by faith alone. It is very important to remember that Van Til as a presuppositional apologetician was very critical of Lutheran theology as a whole. However, he argued that justification by faith alone was a Protestant Reformation consensus between Luther and Calvin, which is a classical understanding of historical theology:

> But if Pascal and many others in the Roman Catholic Church in the Middle Ages enjoyed certainty of faith because of their trust in Christ, it was not till Luther came that Christian people in general did really and fully enter into the joy of sins forgiven, and of assurance of adoption into the family of God through Christ their Savior. Since the Christ of the Scriptures was the object of their faith, this Christ was for the Reformers the source of peace with God and assurance of acceptance with him. There is now no more condemnation for them which are in Christ Jesus.[25]

When we evaluate Van Til's writing and theology, we need to pay special attention to those places where he makes a close connection between salvation as God's pure gift and justification by faith alone, referring to

---

[25] Cornelius Van Til, *The Great Debate Today* (Nutley, NJ: Presbyterian and Reformed Publishing Co., 1971), 96.

Pauline passages such as Romans 4:1-3, 5-7, and 5:1. Moreover, he did not mix works and faith in his discussion of justification by faith, locating Luther and Calvin in the same plane:

> Such was the conviction which Luther and Calvin, going back to Paul, wrought in the hearts of the people of God. It was for this faith that many of those people were willing and able to undergo the martyr's death....
>
> By grace are ye saved, it is the gift of God! That was the refrain of the preaching of the Reformers and of those who followed after them. It was the covenant of grace established with Abraham which became directly or indirectly the theme of many a Reformation sermon, especially on the part of those who followed Calvin. "What shall we say then that Abraham our father, as pertaining to the flesh, hath found? For if Abraham were justified by works, he hath whereof to glory; but not before God. For what saith the scripture? Abraham believed God, and it was counted unto him for righteousness.... Even as David also describeth the blessedness of man, unto whom God imputeth righteousness without works, saying, Blessed are they whose iniquities are forgiven, and whose sins are covered.... Therefore being justified by faith we have peace with God, through our Lord Jesus Christ."
>
> And was not Abraham the father of the faithful? It is not because his life was perfect, or nearly perfect, but because of the faith wrought in his heart by the Spirit of God, that he became the father of the faithful.[26]

Van Til did not argue that Abraham was justified by the obedience of faith or faithfulness as Shepherd has consistently argued. He safeguarded justification by faith alone, making the distinction between works and faith that is the classical understanding of the Pauline concept of justification. In that sense, Van Til rightly observed that Abraham's faithfulness was the fruit of his justifying faith. Therefore, Robbins's claim that Van Til was the father of Shepherd's new theology must be rejected.

Similarly, Bavinck's theology has nothing to do with Shepherd's monocovenantalism. Bavinck clearly maintained the distinction between Law and Gospel in his exposition of justification by faith alone and

---

[26] Ibid., 96-7.

salvation by grace alone. He embraced both union with Christ and the distinction between Law and Gospel in his formulation of justification by faith alone. In that regard, his theology is profoundly Reformational and Pauline:

> Hence, too, Paul states very forcefully that in the gospel the righteousness of God is revealed (Rom. 1:17 and 3:21-26). The oneness and the correspondence of the law and the gospel come out in the fact that the righteousness of God is revealed in both. And the difference comes out in the fact that in the law that righteousness is manifested according to the rule, The man who does these things shall live, where as in the gospel that righteousness is revealed without the law and according to the rule, He who, not by works, but by faith in Him who justifies the wicked, believes, he shall have his faith counted to him for righteousness (Rom. 4:5). In the law one's own, perfect, adequate righteousness is required; in the gospel a perfect and adequate righteousness is granted by God through grace in Christ. Inasmuch as man could not and did not want to maintain the justice of God as embodied in His law, God Himself by the gift of righteousness in Christ restored and confirmed His justice. He puts His love and mercy in the service of His righteousness. By giving Himself He fulfills His own law. And in grace He counts the righteousness of Christ as ours, so that we should fulfill to the full the justice of His law, should receive complete remission of all our sins, and obtain a confident entry into His heavenly kingdom.[27]

Bavinck clearly maintained an absolute distinction between justification by works and justification by faith. He rightly argued that the two principles are diametrically opposed to one another in the Pauline concept of justification. It is a conspicuously lacking idea in Shepherd and the Union with Christ School scholars who exclusively emphasize the union with Christ without maintaining a distinction between works and faith:

---

[27] Herman Bavinck, *Our Reasonable Faith: A Survey of Christian Doctrine*, trans. Henry Zylstra (Grand Rapids, MI: Baker Book House, 1977), 456-57.

*And we know that Paul puts it as bluntly as possible that the justification which now takes place in the gospel through faith is diametrically opposed to all justification by the works of the law.* [Emphasis added] Moreover, this presentation of the matter is interchanged sometimes with that other, according to which justification through faith is regarded as a justification through grace, and accordingly something which excludes all glorying and merit (Rom. 3:24; 4:4ff.; and Tit. 3:5).[28]

Likewise, Bavinck never fell into monocovenantalism in his exposition of covenant and justification by faith and other related theological issues. Simply put, he is the best theological mind ever to emerge from the Dutch Reformed tradition. Bavinck carefully distinguished between justification and sanctification, implying the antithesis between Law and Gospel as well as between works and faith in his soteriology. He also beautifully embraced all the soteriological benefits within the category of union with Christ. This profound balance is completely lost in Shepherd and his supporters. In short, the brilliant theology of Bavinck has nothing to do with the Union with Christ School that has been promoted by Shepherd and his supporters. If Shepherd and his supporters had carried on Bavinck's profound theological tradition, there would never have been theological controversy on covenant and justification by faith at Westminster Seminary in Philadelphia and the Orthodox Presbyterian Church. Bavinck portrays his understanding of union with Christ as follows:

All the same, though it is of the greatest importance to see clearly the distinction between justification and sanctification and to maintain it purely, these two benefits are never separated from each other, not even for a moment. In the counsel of God they are not separated, for justification is one but link in the chain of salvation. Whom God foreknew, He also predestinated, them He also called; and whom He called, them He also justified; and whom He justified, them He also glorified (Rom. 8:29-30). They are not separated either in the person and the work of Christ; for righteousness is not something that lies outside of Christ and be accepted apart from His person. Christ Himself is our

---

[28] Ibid., 460.

righteousness, and He is at the same time our wisdom, sanctification, and redemption (1 Cor. 1:30).[29]

The quotation above demonstrates that Bavinck embraced all the spiritual and soteriological blessings from foreknowledge to glorification under the rubric of union with Christ. However, Bavinck never confounded justification and sanctification. He carefully safeguarded justification by faith alone in light of the antithesis between works and faith, and Law and Gospel. In that sense, Bavinck would never support Shepherd's new theology as Reformational, Confessional, or Pauline, as Gaffin and other supporters have falsely done.

Here, it is worth noting Rowland Ward's comment on Shepherd and Gaffin. Evaluating Shepherd's view on covenant and justification, he locates Shepherd's theology as "the Barthian/Torrance school":

> He wants to stress God's covenant and faithfulness in it, obedience which is never meritorious. Shepherd's thought, like Stam's, is underpinned by the idea that any concept of works or merit in the covenant relationship, whether with Adam, Christ or believers, is alien to Scripture and essentially self-righteous/legalistic in nature. In this respect his position is like the Barthian/Torrance school. It is perhaps significant that Shepherd did some studies under Berkouwer.[30]

It is interesting, however, that Ward identifies Gaffin's theology in the line of Bavinck and Vos, while he identifies Shepherd's theology in the line of Barthian theology:

> Kline's positions have been championed by Mark W. Karlberg, but his contribution has been blunted by misplaced argument and very personal attacks on others, particularly Norman Shepherd and those perceived to sympathize with the latter's position .... Dr Richard Gaffin's position is in fact in the line of H. Bavinck and G. Vos, as is my own.[31]

---

[29] Ibid., 461.
[30] Ward, *God & Adam*, 189.
[31] Ibid., 184-85.

I disagree. I do not think that Bavinck and Vos would ever defend Shepherd's new theology as Reformational and Pauline. Their theology does not know the monocovenantalism into which Shepherd and Gaffin radically fall. In that sense, Ward's separation between Shepherd and Gaffin is an incorrect assessment. As a matter of fact, it is simply unfair to Shepherd or Gaffin. Ward is too prejudiced to identify Shepherd's theology as Barthiansm, while he identifies Gaffin with Bavinck and Vos. Certainly, there is not even a hint of monocovenantalism in Bavinck and Vos, while Gaffin has promoted eschatological monocovenantalism, exclusively emphasizing union with Christ in the *ordo salutis*.

## E. Recapitulation

As Shepherd distorts Calvin's theology, injecting his monocovenantalism into it, he also distorts Paul's theology from the same perspective. However, we must notice that Shepherd is correct in saying that the Palestine Judaism at the time of Paul believed in legalistic righteousness and salvation. Here, he disagrees with the New Perspective on Paul exponents, although both agree with the idea that there is no distinction between Law and Gospel in Paul's soteriology. Unfortunately, his monocovenantalism does not allow the reading that Paul proclaimed justification by faith alone but "by a penitent and obedient faith." Here, Shepherd not only destroys Calvin's soteriology, but Paul's soteriology as well:

> There is a vast difference between the works of the law that Paul everywhere condemns and *the obedience of faith* [Emphasis added] that Paul everywhere commends and encourages. In the language of the prophet Micah, it is the difference between ten thousand of rivers of oil (works of the law and much more!) and doing justice, loving mercy, and walking humbly with your God (Mic. 6:7, 8). Therefore, Paul does not come into conflict with himself when he declares that *justification comes by a penitent and obedient faith, and not by works of the law.* [Emphasis added][32]

---

[32] Shepherd, "Justification by Faith in Pauline Theology," 100.

We have to notice that Shepherd alters the classical Pauline usage, "faith" into "the obedience of faith." He interchangeably uses "the obedience of faith," and "a penitent and obedient faith" instead of justification by faith alone. In that sense, Shepherd's penitent and obedient faith hermeneutics is almost identical to Daniel Fuller's obedience of faith hermeneutics where the classical distinction between Law and Gospel is clearly rejected. It is the main reason that those who follow and support Shepherd's new theology are adopting Daniel Fuller's hermeneutics uncritically as we see among Reformed theonomists.

In Shepherd's new theology, he exclusively emphasizes 'union with Christ' (*unio cum Christo*) as a hermeneutical tool to interpret the doctrine of justification by faith, and justification and sanctification are ultimately indistinguishable. In doing so, Shepherd again misinterprets Calvin's concept of 'double grace' wherein Calvin makes a clear distinction between justification and sanctification, though he embraces them within the category of union with Christ. To be sure, Calvin was irrefutably clear that when he discussed the doctrine of justification by faith alone; he referred it to the antithesis between works and faith along with union with Christ. However, Shepherd and other Union with Christ School scholars do not read correctly Calvin's concept of "double grace," exclusively emphasizing union with Christ. Again, Shepherd portrays Calvin as though he was a neo-legalist in his depiction of "double grace." He falsely portrays Calvin as though he belonged to or was a member of the Union with Christ School, represented by such as Gaffin, Frame, Lillback, Ferguson, and others:

> Justification and sanctification in union with Christ summarize what belongs to the essence of my salvation. Justification and sanctification are what Calvin called the "double grace" that we receive through union with Christ (*Institutes*, 3/11/1). United to Christ I am justified and sanctified. Jesus saves us by destroying both the guilt and the corruption of sin. That is to say he saves us by forging our sins and by transforming us so that we become righteous persons. Those who are forgiven and who are transformed into covenant keepers are the righteous who will inherit eternal life.[33]

---

[33] Ibid.

Frame's remark on his support of Shepherd's new theology as evangelical and Reformed is quite startling. Certainly, Shepherd clearly denies the imputation of the righteousness of active obedience of Christ in the arena of justification. He plainly denies the antithesis between Law and Gospel in the arena of justification and salvation, which is the classical understanding of the Protestant Reformation and a Pauline idea. His radical new interpretation is anti-Reformational, anti-Reformed, and anti-Pauline. Frame does not acknowledge that Paul in Galatians teaches that anyone who mixes Law and Gospel and works and faith in the arena of justification by faith and salvation falls into "another gospel" (*heteron euangelion*). Paul was the apostle of love, but he had no sympathy for Judaizers, who were introducing neo-legalism in Galatian churches (Gal. 1:6-10). Frame in his support to Shepherd's new theology misinterprets not only historical theology, especially Reformed theology, but also Pauline soteriology in a similar manner to Shepherd:

> I hope that Shepherd's more vehement critics will listen to his words in this volume. Shepherd teaches that "the sin of Adam plunged the whole human race into sin, condemnation, and death" (Chapter 6). How does God redeem us from this awful condition? Shepherd says,
>
>> Salvation comes ultimately through Jesus Christ who does two things: he deals definitively with the guilt of sin, and he deals definitively with the corruption of sin. By his death and resurrection he pays the penalty for sin and on this ground bestows the gift of forgiveness. This is justification. By his death and resurrection he destroys the corruption of sin so that we are recreated in righteousness and holiness. This is sanctification. Those who are justified and sanctified in union with Christ are the righteous who will inherit the kingdom and enter into eternal life. (Chapter 6)
>
> This is clearly a biblical, evangelical, and Reformed understanding of the gospel and nothing else. It is so plain that frankly I find it hard to credit the intelligence or spiritual perception of anyone who objects to it. I am hoping that readers will take these words seriously. There is certainly room for disagreement with his broader discussion. But no one, I think, can legitimately doubt that he has the gospel straight.[34]

---

[34] Sandlin ed., *Backbone of the Bible*, xi.

Similarly, Gaffin, as a leading Pauline scholar of the Union with Christ School especially in respect to Pauline soteriology, suggests that justification by faith must be seen exclusively in relation to the concept of union with Christ. In Gaffin's reading of the Pauline doctrine of justification, there is no place for justification by faith alone in light of a complete antithesis between works and faith:

> If anything, this outlook which makes justification exponential of existential union with the resurrected Christ serves to keep clear what preoccupation with the idea of imputation can easily obscure, namely, that the justification of the ungodly is not arbitrary but according to truth: it is synthetic with respect to the believer only because it is analytic with respect to Christ (as resurrected). *Not justification by faith but union with the resurrected Christ by faith (of which union, to be sure, the justifying aspect stands out perhaps most prominently) is the central motif of Paul's applied soteriology.* [Emphasis added][35]

Likewise, Shepherd and other Union with Christ School scholars exclusively emphasize union with Christ in the discussion of justification by faith, ignoring and rejecting the implication of complete antithesis between works and faith. Precisely, here, they depart from the Protestant Reformation and Pauline soteriology. As a result, their view of justification inevitably falls into neo-legalism whereby they mix faith and works. However, Paul clearly taught justification by faith alone, excluding any kind of works in its formulation. Calvin and Reformed theology subsequently affirmed justification by faith alone, interpreting that in light of the complete antithesis between works and faith.

## F. Romans 2:13

Paul self-consciously applied the antithesis between Law and Gospel when he discussed his soteriology, especially in respect to justification by faith and salvation by grace. Calvin and the latter Reformed theologians rightly interpreted justification by faith alone in light of the antithesis between Law

---

[35] Gaffin, *Resurrection and Redemption*, 132.

and Gospel although they embraced it within the category of union with Christ. Calvin and the orthodox Reformed theologians self-consciously applied the antithesis between Law and Gospel as a hermeneutical tool to interpret justification by faith alone as Paul did after his conversion experience at the Damascus Road.

Unfortunately, Shepherd and other Union with Christ School scholars at Westminster Seminary in Philadelphia self-consciously abandoned the antithesis between Law and Gospel in their interpretation of justification by faith. And obviously, they fall into covenantal legalism where they inevitably introduce sinner's covenantal obedience into the arena of justification by faith.

A radical difference among Calvin and Shepherd and Union with Christ School scholars has been found in the interpretation and its implication to justification by faith where Paul says, "For it is not those who hear the law who are righteous in God's sight, but it is those who obey the law who will be declared righteous" (Rom. 2:13).

One of the best possible hermeneutical options may be that Paul states a hypothetical way of salvation and justification through perfect obedience to the law, which is an impossible way to do so as totally depraved sinners in the first Adam. So, the law ultimately leads to the last Adam, who really and covenantally fulfilled all the requirements of the law through his entire perfect life and atoning death. Calvin brilliantly observed Paul's argument of a hypothetical way of justification by works, which is an impossible task as sinners. In that sense, Calvin interprets this verse in light of "Do this and you will live" in Deuteronomy 18:5, which is a classical biblical passage for the antithesis between Law and Gospel:

This anticipates an objection which the Jews might have adduced. As they had heard that the law was the rule of righteousness, (Deut. iv.1,) they gloried in the mere knowledge of it: to obviate this mistake, he declares that the hearing of the law or any knowledge of it is of no such consequence, that any one should on that account lay claim to righteousness, but that works must be produced, according to this saying, "He who will do these shall live in them." The import then of this verse is the following, - "That if righteousness besought from the law, the law must be fulfilled; for the righteousness of the law consists in the perfection of works." They who pervert this passage for the purpose of building up justification by works, deserve most fully to be laughed at even by children.[36]

Calvin rightly interpreted Romans 2:13 from the perspective of the principle of justification by works. And it is the 'pedagogical use of the law' (*usus paedagogicus legis*) or the second use of the law, which ultimately leads to Christ, who met the requirement of justification by works:

> For the Apostle only urges here on the Jews what he had mentioned, the decision of the law, - That by the law they could not be justified, except they fulfilled the law, that if they transgressed it, a curse was instantly pronounced on them. Now we do not deny but that perfect righteousness is prescribed in the law: but as all are convicted of transgression, we say that another righteousness must be sought. Still more, we can prove from this passage that no one is justified by works; for if they alone are justified by the law who fulfill the law, it follows that no one is justified; for no one can be found who can boast of having fulfilled the law.[37]

Likewise, Calvin brilliantly interprets Romans 2:13 in light of the antithesis between Law and Gospel, classically understood to be the hermeneutical and theological background of justification by faith alone. Of course, Shepherd takes a monocovenantal road where he rejects the distinction between Law and Gospel in relation to justification by faith alone. As such, in referring to Romans 2:13, he argues that believers' final justification will be by "the obedience of faith," which is a clear denial of the once for all nature of the forensic nature of justification by faith alone, excluding any kind of works or obedience:

> In the language of Romans 2, those who are seeking to be justified and saved by the works of the law do not keep the law. They only hear the law; they do not do what it says. In contrast to that inconsistency, Paul describes true believers as those who repent of sin and who seek to do what is good according to God's law. They are recreated in Christ for this very purpose and they will inherit eternal life. Romans 2:13 says,

---

[36] Calvin, *Commentaries on the Epistle to the Romans*, 2:13.
[37] Ibid.

'For it is not those who hear the law who are righteous in God's sight, but it is those who obey the law who will be declared righteous.' *That obedience is the obedience of faith. Those who believe in Jesus with this kind of faith will be justified.* [Emphasis added] Paul says in verse 16, 'This will take place on the day when God will judge men's secrets through Jesus Christ, as my gospel declares.'[38]

Gaffin's argument in respect to final or eschatological justification is somewhat different from Shepherd. Gaffin, as a Pauline scholar, emphasizes the eschatological tension between already but not yet in his description of the Pauline soteriology. His emphasis on the Pauline eschatological tension between already but not yet is a concrete idea in and of itself. However, Gaffin pushes too far when he applies the Pauline eschatological tension in the doctrine of justification. Of course, Gaffin's eschatological tension in his doctrine of justification is driven by his rejection of the distinction between Law and Gospel, which is absolutely essential for justification by faith alone:

> For justification, it is fair to say that in general Reformation theology has grasped, at least intuitively, the eschatological 'already' emphatically asserted, for instance, in Romans 5:1 and 8:1. But it has been much more inhibited, no doubt because of polemics with Rome, in recognizing, and incorporating in its doctrinal formulations, the still future aspect of justification also taught in the New Testament (e.g., Rom 2:6-13; Gal 5:5-6). The Westminster Catechisms, for instance, confess that believers will be 'openly acknowledged and acquitted in the day of judgment'; such language is thoroughly forensic. But integral tie between that future acquittal and present justification needs to be made clear; as a *single* justification by faith, the one is the consummation of the other. *For now until Jesus comes, the believer's justification is most certainly settled but not 'storm free.'* [Emphasis added] Faith, as justifying, must persevere in love (Gal 5:6). No doubt the proverbial razor's edge between the truth of the gospel and serious error presents itself here (as so often in our theologizing), a narrow ledge that will have to be negotiated with care.[39]

---

[38] Shepherd, "Justification by Faith in Pauline Theology," 94.
[39] Gaffin, "The Vitality of Reformed Dogmatics," 34.

As such, Gaffin's interpretation of the Pauline eschatology establishes a tension between already but not yet even in the doctrine of justification by faith. In doing so, he inevitably denies the once for all nature of the forensic justification by faith alone in the milieu of the distinction between Law and Gospel.

N.T. Wright, as an exponent of New Perspective on Paul, rejects the Pauline distinction between Law and Gospel as we have already discussed. Like Gaffin, he applies the Pauline eschatology of already but not yet into the arena of the forensic understanding of justification by faith. However, the theological problem in Wright's wording is much more visible than with Gaffin. Wright establishes significantly a great tension between present justification by faith and final justification by works in his analysis on Romans 2:13 and subsequent passages such as Romans 2:14-16; 3:24-26; 8:9-11:

> Present justification declares, on the basis of faith, what future justification will affirm publicly (according to 2:14-16 and 8:9-11) on the basis of the entire life. And in making this declaration (3:26), God himself is in the right, in that he has been faithful to the covenant; he has dealt with sin, and upheld the helpless; and in the crucified Christ he has done so impartially. The gospel – not 'justification by faith,' but the message about Jesus – thus reveals the righteousness, that is, the covenant faithfulness, of God.[40]

Wright's implication of the Pauline eschatological tension between already but not yet into the arena of the forensic justification is a good example why those who have been influenced by the Union with Christ scholars in rejecting the distinction between Law and Gospel, began to adopt the New Perspective on Paul.


## G. The Redefinition of Justification by Faith Alone

As we have observed so far, Shepherd and his supporters, the Union with Christ School scholars, have undermined any hermeneutical and

---

[40] Wright, *What Saint Paul Really Said*, 129.

theological ground to affirm justification by faith alone. *Sola fide* was both correctly interpreted and promoted by the Protestant Reformers, including Calvin, and was beautifully set forth in the Westminster Standards as a confessional statement. Shepherd, however, radically reinterprets the Confessional formulation according to a radical monocovenantalism in which he rejects the antithesis between Law and Gospel. In doing so, he and his supporters undermine the crucial importance of the antithesis between Law and Gospel in understanding of justification by faith alone in the Westminster Standards. Interestingly, Shepherd argues that the Confessional statement in respect to faith as the sole instrument of justification does not mean that it affirms justification by faith alone:

> There are only two places in the Westminster Standards where the expression 'faith alone' is used. One of these is in the Larger Catechism, Question and Answer 70.
>
>> What is justification? Justification is an act of God's free grace unto sinners, in which he pardoneth all their sins, accepteth and accounteth their persons righteous in his sight; not for anything wrought in them, or done by them, but only for the perfect obedience and full satisfaction of Christ, by God imputed to them, and received by faith alone.
>
> The other is the Shorter Catechism, Question and Answer 33.
>
>> What is justification? Justification is an act of God's free grace, wherein he pardoneth all our sins, and accepteth us as righteous in his sight, only for the righteousness of Christ imputed to us, and received by faith alone.
>
> The thought is the same in both answers and corresponds to what we find in the Confession. When the Catechisms say that imputed righteousness is received by faith alone they are describing the instrumental function of faith. They do not use the formula, "justified by faith alone."[41]

---

[41] Shepherd, "Justification by Faith Alone," 78.

Shepherd undermines the significance of the affirmation of justification by faith alone in the Westminster Standards. In fact, justification by faith alone and faith as the sole instrument of justification are coterminous in the Confessional formulation.

The Westminster divines self-consciously stated that the soteric blessings of justification are received "by faith alone." This reflects a careful adaptation of the Pauline antithesis between works and faith in relation to justification by faith, and is also why the Westminster divines make reference to Galatians 2:16 and Philippians 3:9, noticing the antithetical character of works and faith in the Pauline doctrine of justification. Therefore, it is worthy to quote the Westminster divines' biblical reference on faith alone to demonstrate how Shepherd misinterprets the Confessional formulation of justification by faith alone:

> Gal. 2:16. Knowing that a man is not justified by the works of the law, but *by the faith of Jesus Christ,* even we have believed in Jesus Christ, that we might be *justified by the faith of Christ,* and not by the works of the law: for by the works of the law shall no flesh be justified. Phil. 3:9. And be found in him, not having mine own righteousness, which is of the law, but *that which is through the faith of Christ, the righteousness which is of God by faith.*[42]

Contrastingly, Shepherd radically reinterprets the Confessional formula "faith" as "the alone instrument of justification" as stated in the statement, which is not necessarily the affirmation of justification by faith alone. Likewise, Shepherd radically reinterprets the Confessional statement in respect to justification "by faith alone" in light of his radical monocovenantalism, collapsing works and faith:

> We can discover some good reasons in the Westminster Confession itself to explain why it might be inappropriate, though not impossible, for the Confession to say explicitly that justification is by faith alone.

---

[42] It is quoted from the Larger Catechism Answer 72 biblical reference number 44 and the Shorter Catechism Answer 33 biblical reference number 12.

The first reason is found in chapter 11, section 2, itself. After making the point that faith is the alone instrument of justification the Confession goes on to say that this faith is, as a matter of fact, never alone.

> Faith, thus receiving and resting on Christ and His righteousness, is the alone instrument of justification: yet is it not alone in the person justified, but is ever accompanied with all other saving graces, and is no dead faith, but worketh by love.

> The faith that is the alone instrument of justification is not alone and it never is alone. It is ever accompanied with all the other saving graces. It is not a dead faith but a faith that works by love.[43]

Similarly, Shepherd uses the Westminster Confession of Faith 11:2 as the statement that the Confession actually does not affirm the classical statement of justification by faith alone. It is another example that Shepherd self-consciously reinterprets the Confessional formulation of justification by faith in light of his monocovenantalism where he rejects the distinction between works and faith along with the distinction between Law and Gospel. His monocovenantalism does not allow it.

Here, we need to be reminded that the Westminster divines depicted faith as "the alone instrument of justification" in order to affirm justification by faith alone in light of the Pauline antithesis between works and faith. On the other hand, the Westminster divines stated that "yet is it [faith] not alone in the person justified, but is ever accompanied with all other saving graces" to demonstrate that good works and other soteriological blessings must be accompanied in light of union with Christ. However, the major problem with Shepherd's interpretation on the Confessional view of justification is that he does not use the antithesis between works and faith, only applying the concept of union with Christ in a confusing and destructive manner.

We have to understand that the Westminster divines did not formulate the doctrine of justification by faith alone in light of monocovenantalism where Shepherd radically falls into. They self-consciously applied the concept of union with Christ to embrace all the soteriological blessings,

---

[43] Shepherd, "Justification by Faith Alone," 79.

including justification and sanctification, while they made a careful distinction between works and faith to denote the biblical doctrine of justification by faith alone:

> Q. 69. What is the communion in grace which the members of the invisible church have with Christ?
> A. *The communion in grace which the members of the invisible church have with Christ, is their partaking of the virtue of his mediation, in their justification, adoption, sanctification, and whatever else, in this life, manifests their union with him.* [Emphasis added]
> Q. 71. How is justification an act of God's free grace?
> A. Although Christ, by his obedience and death, did make a proper, real, and fully satisfaction to God's justice in the behalf of them that are justified; *yet in as much as God accepteth the satisfaction from a surety, which he might have demanded of them, and did provide this surety, his own only Son, imputing his righteousness to them, and requiring nothing of them for their justification but faith, which also is his gift, their justification is to them of free grace.* [Emphasis added][44]

As such, the Westminster divines affirmed justification by faith alone in light of the distinction between works and faith while all the soteric blessing are embraced by the concept of union with Christ. In short, the Westminster divines did not use the important hermeneutical tool, union with Christ, to mix works and faith in the forensic understanding of justification as Shepherd and his supporters.

---

[44] Larger Catechism, Q & A. 69, 71.

# III.
## The Covenant Way of Salvation

Reformed hermeneutics and theology rightly followed Calvin's hermeneutical and theological tradition. In that sense, covenant hermeneutics and theology after the pattern of Calvin never confused justification and sanctification, although both are included within the comprehensive concept of 'union with Christ' (*unio cum Christo*). Unfortunately, Shepherd's concept of the covenant way of salvation confuses justification and sanctification, both being radically reinterpreted by a distorted concept of union with Christ. Shepherd proposes a new way of salvation, which may be a harmonized concept that seeks to solve an assumed dilemma between Paul's soteriology and James 2:14. He argues that his proposal about the covenant way of salvation may be a concrete biblical answer to the Roman Catholic concept of the meritorious understanding of salvation:

> Roman Catholic teaching is faulty on two related but distinct levels. On one level, Rome's doctrine of salvation requires that place be given to human merit. This is clear from the decrees of the Council of Trent. But if there is place for human merit, then there is place for boasting about meritorious achievement. However, Paul says in Ephesians 2:8-9, 'For it is by grace you have been saved, through faith – and this not from your

selves, it is the gift of God – not by works, so that no one can boast.' Our boast must be in the work of God, so that no one can boast.'[1]

Interestingly, Shepherd's concept of the covenant way of salvation includes faith, repentance, and obedience as the way of salvation while he rejects the Roman Catholic notion of meritorious way of salvation:

> But on a deeper level, what must be challenged in the Roman Catholic doctrine is the very idea of merit itself. God does not, and never did, relate to his people on the basis of a works/merit principle. The biblical texts to which Rome appeals must be read in the light of the covenant. Then the biblical demands for repentance and obedience, together with the warnings against disobedience, can be seen for what they are. They are not an invitation to achieve salvation by human merit. They are a call to find salvation wholly and exclusively in Jesus Christ through faith in him. It is the biblical doctrine of covenant that challenges Roman Catholicism at its root.[2]

However, Shepherd's rejection of the Roman Catholic concept of a meritorious way of salvation in light of covenant perspective introduces believers' repentance and obedience as the covenant way of salvation, an idea which is alien to Calvin and the Reformed covenant theology. He argues that his covenant way of salvation is a covenantal solution between Roman Catholic legalism and evangelical antinomianism:

> The answer to this dilemma is to be found in the doctrine of the covenant, with its two parts, promise and obligation. In keeping with his eternal purpose, the Lord God brings us into covenant with himself. All of the blessings of the covenant are ours as gifts of sovereign grace. The covenantal demand for faith, repentance, and obedience is simply the way in which the Lord leads us into possession of these blessings.
>
> Salvation is both by *grace* and through *faith*. These are the two parts of the covenant: grace and faith, promise and obligation. Grace is not without conditions, and a living and active faith is not meritorious

---

[1] Shepherd, *The Call of Grace*, 60.
[2] Ibid., 60-61.

achievement. It is the biblical doctrine of covenant that enables us to sail safely between the Scylla of legalism and the Charybdis of antinomianism.[3]

Of course, Shepherd's emphasis on covenantal obedience is a vitally important biblical idea in believers' life. However, he fails to locate covenantal obedience within the context of the believer's progressive sanctification. This failure again is a logical hermeneutical and theological consequence of the rejection of the Law and Gospel distinction in Shepherd's hermeneutics and theology. Unlike Shepherd, Calvin did not confuse justification and sanctification. In Calvin's theology, justification by faith alone and salvation by grace alone are closely tied, and stand and fall together:

> Therefore, in the passage cited above, to prove that we have attained the hope of salvation by his grace alone, not by works [cf. Eph. 2:8-9], he states that "we are his creatures, since we have been reborn in Christ Jesus for good works, which God prepared beforehand that we should walk in them" [Eph. 2:10, cf. Vg.]. …. *By this confession we deprive man of all righteousness, even to the slightest particle, until, by mercy alone, he is reborn into the hope of eternal life, since if the righteousness of works brings anything to justify us, we are falsely said to be justified by grace.* [Emphasis added] Obviously, the apostle was not forgetful when he declared justification free, since he proves in another passage that grace would no longer grace if works availed [Rom. 11:6].[4]

We need to be reminded that Calvin's soteriological idea of justification by faith alone and salvation by grace alone is closely interrelated with Paul's soteriology. In fact, Paul states that salvation by grace alone and through faith alone as we read it "for *by grace [chariti]* you have been saved *through faith [dia pisteos]*; and that not of yourselves, it is the gift of God" (Eph. 2:8, *NASB*). Likewise, Calvin rightly excludes any kind of human obedience in sinner's justification and salvation in his exposition of Ephesians 2:8. In fact, in Calvin's soteriology in the exposition of the

---

[3] Ibid., 63.
[4] Calvin, *Institutes*, 3:14:5.

Pauline soteriology, justification by faith alone, salvation by grace alone and faith alone are coterminous:

> *Having treated of election and of effectual calling, he arrives at this general conclusion, that they had obtained salvation by faith alone.* [Emphasis added] First, he asserts, that the salvation of the Ephesians was entirely the work, the gracious work of God. But then they had obtained this grace by faith. On one side, we must look at God; and, on the other, at man. God declares, that he owes us nothing; so that salvation is not a reward or recompense, but unmixed grace. The next question is, in what way do men receive that salvation which is offered to them by the hand of God? The answer is, *by faith*; and hence he concludes that nothing connected with it is our own. If, on the part of God, it is grace alone, and if we bring nothing but faith, which strips us of all commendation, it follows that salvation does not come from us.[5]

In Calvin's soteriology, salvation is absolutely the sovereign work of God, eliminating any kind of human obedience in its realm. Calvin rightly argued that God alone is the author of salvation:

> When, on the part of man, the act of receiving salvation is made to consist in faith alone, all other means, on which men are accustomed to rely, are discarded. Faith, then, brings empty to God, that he may be filled with the blessings of Christ. And so he adds, *not of yourselves*; that, claiming nothing for themselves, they may acknowledge God alone as the author of their salvation.[6]

It is remarkable how Calvin carefully refuted Papists' meritorious concept of sinner's justification and salvation in his exposition of Ephesians 2:9. Again, in Calvin's soteriology, justification by faith alone and salvation by grace alone are coterminous. Moreover, Calvin interpreted them in light of the Law and Gospel antithesis, which was exemplified by Paul's hermeneutics and soteriology:

---

[5] Calvin, *Commentaries on the Epistle to the Ephesians*, 2:8.
[6] Ibid.

Instead of what he had said, that their salvation is of grace, he now affirms, that "it is the gift of God." Instead of what he had said, "Not of yourselves," he now says, "Not of works." Hence we see, that the apostle leaves nothing to men procuring salvation. In these three phrases, - not of yourselves, - *it is the gift of God*, - *not of Works*, - he embraces the substance of his long argument in the Epistles to the Romans and to the Galatians, that righteousness comes to us from the mercy of God alone, - is offered to us in Christ by the Gospel, without the merit of works.

This passage affords an easy refutation of the idle cavil by which Papists attempt to evade the argument, that we are justified without works. Paul, they tell us, is speaking about ceremonies. But the present question is not confined to one class of works. Nothing can be more clear than this. The whole righteousness of man, which consists in works, - nay, the whole man, and everything that he can call his own, is set aside. We must attend to the contrast between God and man, - between grace and works. Why should God be contrasted with man, if the controversy related to nothing more than ceremonies?[7]

Unlike Calvin, however, Shepherd used the concept of 'union with Christ' to reject justification by faith alone as we have already discussed. In addition, he uses it to reject salvation by faith alone and grace alone, applying the idea of covenantal obedience or conditionality in its arena unlike Calvin and other orthodox Reformed theologians. To be sure, Shepherd's rejection of salvation by grace alone in light of covenantal obedience is consistent with his monocovenantalism where he rejects the antithesis between Law and Gospel:

Salvation comes ultimately through Jesus Christ who does two things: he deals definitely with the guilt of sin, and he deals definitely with the corruption of sin. By his death and resurrection he pays the penalty for sin and on this ground bestows the gift of forgiveness. This is justification. By his death and resurrection he destroys the corruption of sin so that we are recreated in righteousness and holiness. This is sanctification. Those who are justified and sanctified in union with Christ are the righteous who will inherit the kingdom and enter into eternal life.[8]

---

[7] Ibid., 2:9.
[8] Shepherd, "Justification by Works in Reformed Theology," 118.

Shepherd's new theology is confusing because he uses the language of salvation as God's gift while he denies salvation by faith alone and grace alone. Of course, it is the most confusing part of Shepherd's new theology:

> Our salvation from beginning to end is wholly and exclusively the gift of God's sovereign grace. The Lord leads us into possession of eternal life in the way of faith, and this faith is specifically faith in Jesus and his shed blood. Faith in Jesus is ever and always a living and active response to the gospel message. The way of faith is also the way of repentance and obedience because true faith inevitably and invariably expresses itself in faithfulness.[9]

Likewise, Shepherd's exclusive emphasis on union with Christ in his soteriology leads him to deny salvation by faith alone and grace alone although he adopts the language of salvation as the gift of God in his sovereign grace while he rejects the substance of it. We need to be reminded that Shepherd's rejection of salvation by faith alone and grace alone is consistent to his monocovenantal principle where he clearly rejects the antithesis between Law and Gospel along with Christ's meritorious obedience.

I already indicated that Shepherd's rejection of the antithesis between Law and Gospel made him deny the meritorious obedience of Christ, which was firmly affirmed by the Reformers, including Calvin. In relation to this, Shepherd denies justification by faith alone. To be consistent with his hermeneutics and new theology, he denies salvation by grace alone, which was rightly affirmed by Calvin and the latter Reformed orthodox theology, including the Westminster Standards. In that sense, Shepherd's monocovenantal understanding of salvation is radically different from Paul's profound concept of salvation by grace alone.

---

[9] Ibid., 119.

# IV.
## Covenant and Election

In Shepherd's monocovenantalism, the classical understanding of the doctrine of predestination also falls apart. This is not particularly surprising, since the Pauline doctrine of double predestination of divine election and reprobation has been properly understood under the hermeneutical principle of the distinction between Law and Gospel in Calvin and the Reformed theologians since the Protestant Reformation, and as spelled out in the Westminster Standards. The Westminster divines beautifully laid out the doctrine of double predestination, based upon the Pauline passages such as Romans 9:6-23 and Ephesians 1:3-14. According to the Westminster divines, the Pauline doctrine of election must be viewed from the perspective of God's sovereign and free grace, which is rightly understood by the distinction between works and faith, which in itself reflects the distinction between Law and Gospel in the Pauline soteriology and divine election:

> Those of mankind that are predestinated unto life, God, before the foundation of the world was laid, according to His eternal and immutable purpose, and the secret counsel and good pleasure of His will, hath chosen, in Christ, unto everlasting glory, out of his mere free grace and love, without any foresight of faith, or good works, or perseverance in

either of them, or any other thing in the creatures, as conditions, or causes moving Him thereunto: and all to the praise of His glorious grace.[1]

Unlike the proper Pauline statement of the Westminster Standards in respect to the distinction between works and faith to denote the sovereign free grace in the divine election, Shepherd's monocovenantalism does not allow the distinction between works and faith in the divine election and soteriology as he mixes it in the doctrine of justification by faith. To be consistent with his monocovenantalism, Shepherd suggests viewing the divine election primarily from the perspective of covenantal obedience:

> From the perspective of the covenant, there is mystery because we are creatures and God is the Creator. We cannot know God exhaustively. God remains incomprehensible. We can never know God's decree as he knows it, and for that reason we cannot begin to reflect on his salvation from the perspective of the decree, even though our salvation originates in the predestinating love and purpose of God. To look at covenant from the perspective of election is ultimately to yield to the primal temptation to be as God. The proper stance for Adam and for all of us after him is *a covenantal stance of faithful obedience. Only from that perspective can election be understood as grace.* [Emphasis added] Therefore, although from the perspective of covenant there is mystery, there is no dilemma and no paradox or contradiction.[2]

Likewise, Shepherd's understanding of the divine election from the perspective of covenantal obedience is a radical reinterpretation of the biblical doctrine of election, which must be viewed from the perspective of the distinction between Law and Gospel along with works and faith. In this sense, I argue that Shepherd's covenantal understanding of the divine election is indistinguishable with the Arminian understanding of conditional election, which was a logical outcome after the denial of the distinction between Law and Gospel in the doctrine of election and soteriology. It is quite interesting to see that Shepherd's covenantal understanding of divine election is also a misapplication of believers'

---

[1] The Westminster Confession of Faith, 3.5.
[2] Shepherd, *The Call of Grace*, 83.

covenantal obedience. The proper place of covenantal obedience is not in the divine election as Shepherd falsely argues, but in the progressive sanctification in believers' life in Christ.

Furthermore, Shepherd argues that Ephesians 1:1-14 is a classical Pauline passage to read the doctrine of election from the perspective of covenantal obedience or faithfulness. It is quite interesting to observe how Shepherd applies believers' covenantal obedience to the divine election. He falsely connects believers' imperfect obedience to the divine election, which is consistent with his monocovenantalism:

> The first passage is Ephesians 1:1-14. These verses are suffused with covenantal language. The Ephesians are a congregation of the Lord Jesus Christ, enjoying the spiritual blessings of the Lord Jesus Christ, enjoying the spiritual blessings of sanctity of life, adoption to sonship, forgiveness of sins, and the seal of the Holy Spirit. At the same time, all of these blessings are traced back to the predestinating love of God. This accent comes so strongly and so repeatedly at the very beginning of the letter, that Paul may even appear to be writing from the perspective of election. We would then have to understand his letter from that perspective. We would have to look at the covenant in the light of election.
>
> Careful attention to the language of these verses makes clear, however, that precisely the reverse is the case. Paul looks at election from the perspective of covenant. For that reason, predestination is not a theological puzzle, but a cause for gratitude. When Paul says, "He chose us" (v.4), we must ask who "we" are. We could say that they are the saints in Ephesus and the faithful in Christ Jesus (v.1)....
>
> In Ephesians 1, Paul writes from the perspective of observable covenant reality and concludes from the visible faith and sanctity of the Ephesians that they are the elect of God.[3]

Here, we see a consistent pattern of Shepherd's monocovenantalism. He falsely applies believers' covenantal obedience in the arena of justification by faith, and uses it to reject the classical Pauline and Reformation doctrine of justification by faith alone as we have already examined. Similarly, he

---

[3] Ibid., 86-88.

applies believers' covenantal obedience to reject unconditional election, which is a concrete Pauline idea and was remarkably interpreted by Calvin and properly adopted by Reformed theologians.

Calvin rightly argues that election must be free and unconditional, refuting the Sophists' concept of meritorious and conditional election when he exposits Ephesians 1:4:

> The foundation and first cause, both of our calling and of all the benefits which we receive from God, is here declared to be his eternal election. If the reason is asked, why God has called us to enjoy the gospel, why he daily bestows upon us so many blessings, why he opens to us the gate of heaven, –the answer will be constantly found in this principle, that *he hath chosen us before the foundation of the world.* The very time when the election took place proves it to be free; for what could we have deserved, or what merit did we possess, before the world was made? How childish is the attempt to meet this argument by the following sophism! "We were chosen because we were worthy, and because God foresaw that we would be worthy." We were all lost in Adam; and therefore, had not God, through his own election, rescued us from perishing, there was nothing to be foreseen. The same argument is used in the Epistle to the Romans, where, speaking of Jacob and Esau, he says, "For the children being not yet born, neither having done any good or evil, that the purpose of God according to election might stand, not of works, but of him that calleth." (Rom. ix. 11.).[4]

Calvin obviously does not view primarily the divine eternal and free election from the perspective of believers' covenantal obedience, as Shepherd wrongly argues. Rather, Calvin properly views believers' covenantal obedience from the perspective of eternal and free election to emphasize God's sovereign and free grace in the divine election, excluding any kind of human obedience as a condition of election. Therefore, Calvin makes a remarkable theological statement that believers' covenantal obedience is the *fruit* of eternal free election:

---

[4] Calvin, *The Epistle to the Ephesians*, 1:4.

*This leads us to conclude, that holiness, purity, and every excellence that is found among men, are the fruit of election; so that once more Paul expressly puts aside every consideration of merit.* [Emphasis added] If God had forseen in us anything worthy of election, it would have been stated the very opposite of what is here employed, and which plainly means that all our holiness and purity of life flow from the election of God.... *The cause, certainly, is not later than the effect. Election, therefore, does not depend on the righteousness of works, of which Paul here declares that it is the cause.* [Emphasis added][5]

Calvin carefully refuted the Sohpists' meritorious concept of the divine election and salvation in his brilliant exposition on Ephesians 1:5. He argues that there are three causes of believers' salvation, which are the concrete reflection of Calvin's theocentric and Christocentric theology unlike Shepherd's monocovenantalism:

Three causes of our salvation are here mentioned, and a fourth is shortly afterwards added. The efficient cause is *the good pleasure of the will* of God, the material cause is, *Jesus Christ*, and the final cause is, *the praise of the glory of his grace.* Let us now see what he says respecting each.

To the first belongs the whole of the following statement. *God hath predestinated us in himself, according to the good pleasure of his will, unto the adoption of sons, and hath made us accepted by his grace.* In the word *predestinate* we must again attend to the order. We were not then in existence, and therefore there was no merit of ours. The cause of our salvation did not proceed from us, but from God alone....

The material cause both of eternal election, and of the love which is now revealed, is *Christ, the Beloved.* This name is given, to remind us that by him the love of God is communicated to us. Thus he is the well-beloved, in order that we may be reconciled by him. The highest and last end is immediately added, the glorious praise of such abundant grace. Every man, therefore, who hides this glory, is endeavouring to overturn the everlasting purpose of God. Such is the doctrine of Christ, lest the whole glory of our salvation should be ascribed undividedly to God alone.[6]

---

[5] Ibid.
[6] Ibid., 1:5.

As such, Calvin rightly interprets the Pauline doctrine of the divine election. He primarily views it from the perspective of God's sovereign and free grace. The brilliance of Calvin's theology lies in a wonderful harmony between the divine free election and believers' covenantal obedience. Calvin makes a connection between the divine free election and believers' covenantal faithfulness in the process of progressive sanctification in light of 'union with Christ' (*unio cum Christo*):

> We learn also from these words, that election gives no occasion to licentiousness, or to the blasphemy of wicked men who say, "Let us live in any manner we please; for, if we have been elected, we cannot perish." Paul tells them plainly, that they have no right to separate holiness of life from the grace of election; for "whom he did predestinate, them he also called, and whom he called, them he also justified." (Rom. viii. 30). The inference, too, which the Catharists, celestines, and Donatists drew from these words, that we may attain perfection in this life, is without foundation. This is the goal to which the whole course of our life must be directed, and we shall not reach it till we have finished our course.[7]

However, Shepherd's covenantal understanding of the divine election from the perspective of covenant mixes faith and obedience, just as he mixes faith and obedience in his exposition of justification by faith. In that sense, he is consistent in his own monocovenantalism. Unlike Shepherd's monocovenantalism, Calvin rightly does not mix faith and obedience in his exposition of the divine election, just as he does not do it in his exposition of justification by faith alone. Shepherd's monocovenantalism, where he rejects the distinction between Law and Gospel, views divine election and soteriology primarily from the perspective of believer's faith and covenantal obedience. However, Calvin and Reformed theology rightly see divine election and soteriology primarily from the perspective of God's infinite and free grace in Jesus Christ. In Shepherd's new theology, from the very beginning, there is no room for God's sovereign and free grace in the divine election and soteriology.

Unlike Shepherd, Calvin properly locates believers' covenantal obedience in the process of sanctification, saying that it is "the fruit of

---

[7] Calvin, *The Epistle to the Romans*, 1:4.

election." And the divine election is the *cause* of believers' covenantal obedience not vice versa, as we already demonstrated.

However, in Shepherd's monocovenantalism, the proper order of the cause and effect in the divine election is overturned and destroyed. As such, Shepherd mistakenly argues that Jesus's parable about the vine and the branches in John 15:1-8 is to demonstrate the divine election from the perspective of covenant. He ignores that it is a classical passage about believers' bearing fruits in the process of progressive sanctification in Jesus Christ:

> A second passage that is illustrative of the covenant perspective on election is John 15:1-8. Jesus is clearly and unambiguously saying in this passage that he is the vine and that his hearers are branches abiding in him. He exhorts them all to continue abiding in him by bearing fruit, and that means by persevering in faith and obedience. If they do, the Father will see to it that they bear even more fruit. They are at no point cast upon their own resources, because as branches they get their vitality at every point from the vine. On the other hand, if certain branches do not abide in Christ, but deny him and become disobedient, the father will cut them off and destroy them. The passage is a grand exhortation to covenant faithfulness, enveloped in the overflowing grace of Christ.[8]

It is quite remarkable to find that Shepherd's covenantal understanding of the divine election mixes believers' faith and obedience in the divine election as well as in the doctrine of justification by faith as we already critically examined. In this regard, Shepherd's covenantal understanding of election is indistinguishable with the Arminian understanding of conditional election even though he denies the conditional nature of the divine election.

At the heart of the Arminian controversy in the early part of the seventeenth century in Netherlands lies the issue of the distinction between Law and Gospel. Arminius and his followers, known as the Remonstrants, refused to adopt the distinction between Law and Gospel in their depiction of the Pauline soteriology, justification by faith, the divine election, and other closely related theological issues. They inevitably fell

---

[8] Shepherd, *The Call of Grace*, 88-89.

into neo-legalism, mixing faith and evangelical obedience in the doctrine of justification by faith and salvation. Furthermore, their rejection of the antithesis between Law and Gospel in relation to the doctrine of justification by faith made them deny the unconditional nature of the divine election. In this sense, the Shepherd Controversy is very reminiscent of the seventeenth-century Arminian controversy in the Netherlands. In refuting the Remonstrant, the Reformed pastors and theologians who formulated *The Canons of Dort* laid out the unconditional nature of the divine election, expositing the Pauline concept of double predestination. Certainly, it was properly and carefully expounded by Calvin during the Reformation. Like Calvin, the Dort divines interpret and view the divine election primarily not from the perspective of the believers' foreseen faith and obedience but from the divine free grace:

> Article 9: *Election Not Based on Foreseen Faith*
> This same election took place, not **on the basis of** foreseen faith, of the obedience of faith, of holiness, or of any other good quality and disposition, as though it were based on a prerequisite cause or condition in the person to be chosen, but rather **for the purpose** of faith, of the obedience of faith, of holiness, and so on. Accordingly, election is the source of each of the benefits of salvation. Faith, holiness, and the other saving gifts, and at last eternal life itself, flow forth from election as its fruits and effects. As the apostle says, *He chose us* (not because we were, but) *so that we should be holy and blameless before him in love* (Eph. 1:4).[9]

One of the promoters of *Auburn Avenue Theology* or *Federal Vision*, John Barach echoes exactly what Shepherd has argued in his "the covenantal election." He mixes faith and obedience in his discussion of the divine election as Shepherd has done:

> Similarly, from eternity, God chose Israel to be His people. He acted that choice in history at the Exodus. That was when God–in history, but according to His eternal plan–took Israel out of the nations for Himself.

---

[9] The Canons of Dort, Article 9, in *Ecumenical Creeds and Reformed Confessions* (Grand Rapids, MI: CRC Publications, 1988), 124-125.

That choice was unconditional. It was not grounded on anything in Israel herself (Deuteronomy 7:7; cf. 9:4-6). God did not choose Israel *because* she was holy but to *be* holy. Israel is holy because God chose her to be His covenant people.

That was true for the nation and for the individuals in the nation. None of them could escape from his calling by saying that the calling to be holy applied only to the nation. God chose Israel for Himself, but that implies that He also chose each member of Israel to belong to Him. Each one had a special calling and responsibility.

That relationship was established unconditionally. But the covenant relationship itself had conditions. Each member of the covenant was obligated to respond to God in faith and obedience. Some persevered; others apostatized. But even the ones who apostatized were, for a time, among God's chosen people, though God did not predestine them to persevere and inherit eternal glory with Christ.[10]

Barach as a promoter of *Auburn Avenue Theology* echoes exactly Shepherd's covenantal way of election and salvation. In his analysis of the divine election, he fails to make a distinction between the national election of Israel in the Old Testament and personal election among the Old Testament Israelites. His discussion on the covenant relationship also mixes faith and obedience as Shepherd typically has done.

We have seen that Shepherd's monocovenantalism not only affects his understanding of soteriology, rejecting justification by faith alone, but also his understanding of the divine election, where he denies the unconditional nature of the election through his misapplication of believer's covenantal obedience in its arena. Unfortunately, the exponents of Auburn Avenue Theology follow exactly in the footsteps of Shepherd's monocovenantalism in their analysis on justification by faith and the divine election.

---

[10] Beisner ed., *The Auburn Avenue Theology*, 151-52.

# Conclusion

I have argued that the Shepherd Controversy on covenant and justification by faith should not focus on Shepherd's new theology alone. Shepherd and his supporters at the Westminster School should be considered as a distinctive new school. I have also suggested calling it "the Union with Christ School," fundamentally different from the Old Princeton and Old Westminster School. The definite breach came after Murray's retirement in 1966. The distinctive theological character of the Union with Christ School is to ignore or to reject the Pauline antithesis between Law and Gospel in the representation of justification by faith, exclusively emphasizing union with Christ as a hermeneutical tool. Their radical reformulation of covenant and justification by faith is simply incompatible with the Protestant Reformation, Reformed theology, and Pauline soteriology. The Union with Christ School scholars' monocovenantalism has had a devastating impact on the evangelical and Reformed world as we witness it among Reformed theonomists, the Federal Vision exponents, and others who have been influenced directly or indirectly by them.

Once again, we need to be reminded that the good news of the Kingdom of God stands and falls together with justification 'by faith alone' (*sola fide*) and salvation 'by grace alone' (*sola gratia*) in Jesus. This is not an empty slogan or a mere lip service to the Protestant Reformation, both Luther and Calvin alike. Calvin profoundly interpreted justification by faith alone in light of the antithesis between Law and Gospel while he attributed to believers all the spiritual and eschatological blessings under the rubric of 'union with Christ' (*unio cum Christo*), from divine foreknowledge to the eschatological heavenly glorification and inheritance. As such, no one can interpret Calvin's exposition on justification by faith alone and salvation by grace alone without referring to the union with Christ on the one hand, and the antithesis between Law and Gospel on the other. Although there are some theological variations among themselves, Shepherd and his supporters at the Westminster School have unanimously rejected the antithesis between Law and Gospel in their analysis of soteriology, exclusively emphasizing union with Christ. In doing so, they have self-consciously reinterpreted Calvin, the Westminster Standards, and Reformed theology from their monocovenantal perspective. As I have demonstrated here, their injection of monocovenantalism into Reformed theology and Pauline soteriology has had a devastating impact on other scholars, pastors, seminarians, and laypeople who have been influenced by their new theology.

In short, the monocovenantalism of Shepherd and the Union with Christ School scholars have in effect provided a shortcut for their followers that lead to the road to Rome, New Perspective on Paul, Neo-orthodoxy, and other forms of ecumenical theology, all roads where the antithesis between Law and Gospel is commonly rejected.

Time passes, and Shepherd and the original Union with Christ School scholars will begin to fade away from the front line of teaching, writing, and preaching as we move further into the 21st century. Certainly, they are conservative Reformed scholars, who have influenced and nurtured many young scholars, pastors, seminarians, and lay people in many good ways. My only plea to them is to restore the forgotten or rejected hermeneutical and theological tool, which is the distinction between Law and Gospel. It is my sincere hope that Reformed and evangelical scholars in the 21st century may begin to teach the Pauline evangelical distinction between Law and Gospel in hermeneutics and theology. Without it, Reformed and evangelical seminaries and churches will be the prey of the New Perspective on Paul or Rome. Let us take the road to Geneva, proclaiming the good news of the Gospel of Jesus Christ until he returns with the shining Glory of the everlasting heaven.

# Bibliography

## A. Primary Sources

Shepherd, Norman. *The Call of Grace: How the Covenant Illumines Salvation and Evangelism*. Phillipsburg, NJ: Presbyterian & Reformed, 2000.

_____. "The Covenant Context for Evangelism." In *The New Testament Student and Theology*, ed. J. H. Skilton. Phillipsburg, NJ: Presbyterian & Reformed, 1976.

_____. "The Grace of Justification." Originally published February 8, 1979 now at http://www.hornes.org/theologia/content/norman_shepherd/the_grace_of_justification.htm.

_____. "Justification by Faith Alone." *Reformation & Revival Journal* 11/2 (2002): 75-89.

_____. "Justification by Faith in Pauline Theology." In *Backbone of the Bible: Covenant in Contemporary Perspective*, ed. P. Andrew Sandlin. TX: Covenant Media Press, 2004.

_____. "Justification by Works in Reformed Theology." In *Backbone of the Bible: Covenant in Contemporary Perspective*, ed. P. Andrew Sandlin. TX: Covenant Media Press, 2004.

_____. "Law and Gospel in Covenantal Perspective: The Unity of God's Salvific Plan." November 15, 2004 online at http://www.christianculture.com/cgi-local/npublisher/viewnews.cgi?category=3&id=1100539305

_____. "My Understanding of Covenant." on line at www.spindleworks.com/library/CR/shepherd.htm

_____. "The Relation of Good Works to Justification in the Westminster Standards." Westminster Theological Seminary, 1976.

_____. "Thirty-Four Theses on Justification in Relation to Faith, Repentance, and Good Works." Westminster Theological Seminary, 1978.

## B. Secondary Sources

Bahnsen, Greg L. *Theonomy in Christian Ethics: Expanded Edition with Replies to Critics.* 2d. ed. Phillipsburg, New Jersey: Presbyterian and Reformed Publishing Company, 1984.

Barth, Karl. *Church Dogmatics.* 4 vols. trans. G. W. Bromiley. Edinburgh: T.&T. Clark, 1974.

Bavinck, Herman. *Our Reasonable Faith: A Survey of Christian Doctrine.* trans. Henry Zylstra. Grand Rapids: MI: Baker Book House, 1977.

Beisner, E. Calvin ed. *The Auburn Avenue Theology, Pros & Con: Debating the Federal Vision.* Fort Lauderdale: FL: Knox Theological Seminary, 2004.

_____. "The Current Challenge." *Modern Reformation* 13/4 (July/August, 2004): 17-22.

Berkouwer, G.. C. *Sin.* trans. Philip C. Holtrop. Grand Rapids, MI: Eerdmans Publishing Company, 1971.

Calvin, John. *Calvin's Commentaries.* 22 vols. Various Translators. Edinburgh: Calvin Translation Society, 1863. Reprint, Grand Rapids, Michigan: Baker Book House, 1996.

_____. *Institutes of the Christian Religion.* ed. John T. McNeill, trans. Ford Lewis Battles. In *The Library of Christian Classics.* vols. XX-XXI. Philadelphia: The Westminster Press, 1975.

Carpenter, Craig B. "A Question of Union with Christ? Calvin and Trent on Justification." *Westminster Theological Journal* 64/2 (Fall, 2002): 363-86.

Dunn, James D. G.. "The Incident at Antioch (Gal. 2:11-18)." *Journal for the Study of the New Testament* 18 (1983): 3-57.

_____. *Jesus, Paul, and the Law: Studies in Mark and Galatians.* Louisville: Westminster, 1990.

_____. "The Justice of God: A Renewed Perspective on Justification by Faith." *Journal of Theological Studies* 43 (1992), 1-22.

_____. "The New Perspective on Paul." *Bulletin of the John Rylands University Library of Manchester* 65 (1983), 95-122.

_____. "Works of the Law and the Curse of the Law (Galatians 3:10-14)." *New Testament Studies* 31 (1985), 523-42.

_____. "Yet Once More — 'The Works of the Law': A Response." *Journal for the Study of the New Testament* 46 (1992): 99-117.

Ecumenical Creeds and Reformed Confessions. Grand Rapids, MI: CRC Publications, 1988.

Ferguson, Sinclair B. *The Doctrine of the Christian Life in the Teaching of Dr. John Owen [1616-83]: Chaplain to Oliver Cromwell and Sometime Vice Chancellor of the University of Oxford.* Ph.D. diss., University of Aberdeen, 1979.

_____. "John Murray." In *Handbook of Evangelical Theologians,* ed. Walter J. Elwell, 168-181. Grand Rapids, Michigan: Baker Book House, 1993.

_____. *John Owen on the Christian Life*. Carlisle / Edinburgh: The Banner of Truth Trust, 1987.

_____. Review of *The New Testament Student and Theology*, ed. by J.H. Skilton. *The Banner of Truth Magazine* (July/August, 1977), 59-63.

_____. "The Teaching of the Confession." In *The Westminster Confession in the Church Today*, ed. Alasdair I. C. Heron, 28-39. Edinburgh: The Saint Andrews Press, 1982.

Frame, John M. *Apologetics to the Glory of God: An Introduction*. Phillipsburg, New Jersey: Presbyterian and Reformed Publishing Company, 1994.

_____. *Cornelius Van Til: An Analysis of His Thought*. Phillipsburg: New Jersey: Presbyterian and Reformed Publishing Company, 1995.

_____. *The Doctrine of God*. Phillipsburg, New Jersey: P & R Publishing, 2002.

_____. *The Doctrine of the Knowledge of God*. Phillipsburg, New Jersey: Presbyterian and Reformed Publishing Company, 1987.

Fuller, Daniel P. *Gospel and Law: Contrast or Continuum? The Hermeneutics of Dispensationalism and Covenant Theology*. Grand Rapids, Michigan: Eerdmans Publishing Company, 1980.

_____. "The Hermeneutics of Dispensationalism." Th.D. diss., Northern Baptist Theological Seminary, Chicago, Illinois, 1957.

_____. "A Response on the Subjects of Works and Grace." *Presbyterion* 9 (1983): 72-9.

Gaffin, Jr., Richard B. "Biblical Theology and the Westminster Standards." In *The Practical Calvinists: An Introduction to the Presbyterian and Reformed Heritage: In Honor of D. Clair Davis' Thirty Years at Westminster Theological Seminary*, ed. Peter A. Lillback, 425-42. Great Britain: Christian Focus Publications, 2002.

_____. "Biblical Theology and the Westminster Standards." *Westminster Theological Journal* 65 (2003): 165-79.

_____. *Resurrection and Redemption: A Study in Pauline Soteriology*. Th.D. diss., Westminster Theological Seminary, 1969.

_____. *Resurrection and Redemption: A Study in Paul's Soteriology*. Phillipsburg, NJ: P&R Publishing Company, 1987.

_____. "Review Essay: Paul the Theologian." *Westminster Theological Journal* 62 (2000): 121-41.

_____. "The Vitality of Reformed Dogmatics." In *The Vitality of Reformed Theology: Proceedings of the International Theological Congress June 20-24th 1994, Noordwijkerhout, The Netherlands*. eds. J.M. Batteau, J.W. Maris, and K. Veling, 16-50. Kampen: Uitgeverij Kok, 1994.

Godfrey, W. Robert. "Westminster Seminary, the Doctrine of Justification, and the Reformed Confessions." In *The Pattern of Sound Doctrine: Systematic Theology at the Westminster Seminaries: Essays in Honor of Robert B. Strimple*, ed. David VanDrunen, 127-48. Phillipsburg, NJ: P&R Publishing, 2004

Green, Doug. "N.T. Wright–A Westminster Seminary Perspective," March 3, 2004 at http://www.ntwrightpage.com/Green_Westminster_Seminary_Perspective.pdf

Hahn, Scott & Kimberly. *Rome Sweet Home*. San Francisco, CA: Ignatius, 1993.

Horton, Michael. "Déjà Vu All Over Again." *Modern Reformation* 13/4 (July/August, 2004): 23-30.

Jeon, Jeong Koo. *Covenant Theology: John Murray's and Meredith G. Kline's Response to the Historical Development of Federal Theology in Reformed Thought.* Lanham, MD: University Press of America, 2004.

_____. "Covenant Theology and Old Testament Ethics: Meredith G. Kline's Intrusion Ethics." *Kerux* (2002), 3-33.

Karlberg, Mark W. *The Changing of the Guard: Westminster Theological Seminary in Philadelphia.* Unicoi, TN: The Trinity Foundation, 2001.

_____. *Gospel Grace: The Modern-Day Controversy.* Eugene, OR: Wipf & Stock Publishers, 2003.

Kline, Meredith G. "Covenant Theology under Attack." *New Horizons* 15/2 (1994): 3-5.

Lillback, Peter Alan. *The Binding of God: Calvin's Role in the Development of Covenant Theology.* Ph.D. diss., Westminster Theological Seminary, 1985.

_____. *The Binding of God: Calvin's Role in the Development of Covenant Theology.* Grand Rapids, MI: Baker Academic, 2001.

_____. "Calvin's Covenantal Response to the Anabaptist View of Baptism." *Christianity and Civilization* 1 (1982): 185-232.

_____. "Ursinus' Development of the Covenant of Creation: A Debt to Melanchthon or Calvin?" *Westminster Theological Journal* 43 (1981): 247-88.

Linden, David H. Review of "Justification by Faith Alone," by Norman Shepherd. In *Reformation & Revival Journal 11/2* (Spring, 2002) online at http://www.grebeweb.com/linden/shepherd_review.htm.

MacLeod, A. Donald. *W. Stanford Reid: An Evangelical Calvinist in the Academy.* Montreal & Kingston: McGill-Queen's University Press, 2004.

Murray, John. *Collected Writings of John Murray: The Claims of Truth.* vol.1. The Banner of Truth Trust, 1976.

_____. *Collected Writings of John Murray: Select Lectures in Systematic Theology.* vol.2. The Banner of Truth Trust, 1977.

_____. *Collected Writings of John Murray: Life (by Iain H. Murray), Sermons and Reviews.* vol.3. The Banner of Truth Trust, 1982.

_____. *Collected Writings of John Murray: Studies in Theology.* vol.4. The Banner of Truth Trust, 1983.

_____. *Principles of Conduct: Aspects of Biblical Ethics.* Grand Rapids, Michigan: Eerdsmans Publishing Company, 1991.

_____. *Redemption: Accomplished and Applied.* Grand Rapids, Michigan: Eerdsmans Publishing Company, 1989.

Perrin, Nicholas. "A Reformed Perspective on the New Perspective," Review of *Justification and the New Perspectives on Paul: A Review and Response,* by Guy Prentiss Waters. *Westminster Theological Journal* 67 (2005), 381-89.

Piper, John. *Counted Righteous in Christ: Should We Abandon the Imputation of Christ's Righteousness.* Wheaton, Illinois: Crossway Books, 2002.

_____. *Desiring God: Meditations of a Christian Hedonist.* Sisters, Oregon: Multnomah Books, 1996.

_____. *The Justification of God.* Grand Rapids, Michigan: Baker Book House, 1983.

_____. *Love Your Enemies: Jesus' Love Command in the Synoptic Gospels & the Early Christian Paraenesis.* Grand Rapids, Michigan: Baker Book House, 1991.

RCUS. "Report of the Special Committee to Study Justification in Light of the Current Justification Controversy: Presented to the 258th Synod of the Reformed Church of the United States." May 10-13, 2004 online at http://www.trinityrcus.com/Articles/reportshepherd1.htm.

Robbins, John W. *A Companion to the Current Justification Controversy.* Unicoi, TN: The Trinity Foundation, 2003.

Robertson, O Palmer. *The Current Justification Controversy.* Unicoi, TN: The Trinity Foundation, 2003.

Sanders, E. P. "The Covenant as a Soteriological Category and the Nature of Salvation in Palestinian and Hellenistic Judaism." In *Jews, Greeks and Christians: Religious Cultures in Late Antiquity.* eds. Robert Hamerton-Kelly and Robin Scroggs, 11-44. Leiden, 1976.

_____. *Jesus and Judaism.* Philadelphia, Pennsylvania: Fortress Press, 1985.

_____. *Jewish Law from Jesus to the Mishnah: Five Studies.* London: SCM Press / Philadelphia: Trinity Press International, 1990.

_____. *Paul.* Oxford / New York: Oxford University Press, 1992.

_____. *Paul and Palestinian Judaism.* Philadelphia, Pennsylvania: Fortress Press, 1977.

_____. *Paul, the Law and the Jewish People.* Philadelphia, Pennsylvania: Fortress Press, 1983.

Sandlin, P. Andrew. *Backbone of the Bible: Covenant in Contemporary Perspective.* TX: Covenant Media Press, 2004.

Sungenis, Robert A. *Not by Faith Alone: The Biblical Evidence for the Catholic Doctrine of Justification.* Santa Barbara, CA: Queenship Publishing Company, 1997.

Trumper, Tim J. R. "Covenant Theology and Constructive Calvinism." Review of *Covenant Theology: John Murray's and Meredith G. Kline's Response to the Historical Development of Federal Theology in Reformed Thought,* by Jeong Koo Jeon *Westminster Theological Journal* 64/2 (2002), 387-404.

Van Til, Cornelius. *Common Grace and the Gospel.* Phillipsburg, New Jersey: Presbyterian and Reformed Publishing Company, 1972.

_____. "Covenant Theology." In *New 20th-Century Encyclopedia of Religious Knowledge,* ed. J. D. Douglas, 240-41. 2d ed. Grand Rapids, Michigan, 1991.

_____. *The Defense of the Faith.* 3d. ed. Phillipsburg, New Jersey: Presbyterian and Reformed Publishing Company, 1967.

_____. *The Great Debate Today.* Nutley, New Jersey: Presbyterian and Reformed Publishing Company, 1971.

_____. *The Intellectual Challenge of the Gospel.* Phillipsburg, New Jersey: Presbyterian and Reformed Publishing Company, 1980.

_____. *An Introduction to Systematic Theology.* Phillipsburg, New Jersey: Presbyterian and Reformed Publishing Company, 1974.

_____. *The Sovereignty of Grace: An Appraisal of G. C. Berkouwer's View of Dordt.* New Jersey: Presbyterian and Reformed Publishing Company, 1969.

Venema, Cornelis P. Review of *The Binding of God: Calvin's Role in the Development of Covenant Theology.* Texts and Studies in Reformation and Post-Reformation Thought, ed. by Richard M. Muller, by Peter A. Lillback. *Mid-America Journal of Theology* 13 (2002):201-209.

_____. Review of *The Call of Grace: How the Covenant Illuminates Salvation and Evangelism,* by Norman Shepherd. *Mid-America Journal of Theology* 13 (2002):232-248.

Vos, Geerhardus. *The Pauline Eschatology.* Reprint, Phillipsburg, New Jersey: P&R Publishing Company, 1994.

Westminster Seminary California Faculty. "Our Testimony on Justification: A Summary of the Statement from the Faculty of Westminster Seminary California." *Modern Reformation* 13/4 (July/August, 2004): 37

Westminster Theological Seminary Faculty. "Westminster Statement on Justification." Unpublished Doctrinal Statement of Westminster Theological Seminary. May 27, 1980

Wilkins, Steve and Garner, Duane eds. *The Federal Vision.* Monroe, Louisiana: Althanasius Press, 2004.

Wilson, Douglas. *'Reformed' Is Not Enough.* Moscow, ID: Canon Press, 2002.

Wright, N. Thomas. *The Climax of the Covenant: Christ and the Law in Pauline Theology.* Minneapolis, Minnesota: Fortress Press, 1991.

_____. "The Paul of History and the Apostle of Faith." *Tyndale Bulletin* 29 (1978): 61-88.

_____. *What Saint Paul Really Said: Was Paul of Tarsus the Real Founder of Christianity?* Grand Rapids, Michigan: Eerdmans Publishing Company, 1997.

Zens, Robert M. *Professor Norman Shepherd on Justification: A Critique.* Th.M. thesis, Dallas Theological Seminary, 1981.